SPEAKING ILL OF THE DEAD

Jerks in California History

SPEAKING ILL OF THE DEAD

THE DEAD

Jerks in California History

Maxine Cass

Guilford, Connecticut

Copyright © 2012 by Morris Book Publishing, LLC

Text design: Sheryl P. Kober
Project editor: Meredith Dias
Layout artist: Milly Iacono

Library of Congress Cataloging-in-Publication Data is available on file.

ISBN: 978-0-7627-7240-7

Printed in the United States of America

10 9 8 7 6 5 4 3 2 1

Contents

Acknowledgments

My roots are deep in California, with family tales of a Pony Express rider, Wells Fargo Bank as the employer of choice for generations, and at least one grandparent who survived San Francisco's Great Earthquake and Fire in 1906. No one ever mentioned the *other* things, the negative history, the bad guys. Who knew California had a pirate, or that the bad guys' bad deeds may not have been black and white, but shades of grey, making them not completely bad, or, put another way, somewhat nuanced jerks?

Fred Gebhart gave me encouragement and support, as he always has, from the beginning to the end of this book project and our lives together.

Thank you to the memory of my father, Harry Cass, a superb storyteller who could weave a tale of a magical family who built their home and rich and wondrous world from string, glue, and tape, and made their existence as real as breathing.

Panther and Mendo, the talkative feline support team of many years, are beloved cats without whose presence nothing can get written.

Virginia McCarthy, a proud native San Franciscan, is always my book-writing cheerleader.

Steve Giordano is my great friend, fellow writer, and a superb storyteller who, like me, never learned much "real" California history in school—but whose mind is always eager to know more.

Julianne Stein's enthusiasm for life and the written word lent cheer to my task.

Sandra Beezy inspires me to keep physically fit and focused while reminding me that she enjoys reading good books and that it's important to buy books to support the hard-working authors.

I am thankful to friends in Gold Hill, Oregon. Tim Marshall was enthusiastic about this book and its writer, and I was inspired by his wonder at the process. Cindy Oldfield loaned me an older book from her own collection that talked about San Francisco's characters and reminded me that bad *characters* like Dennis Kearney can be *very* interesting. Roger Beckwith recalled stark family memories of the St. Francis Dam Disaster. And Lindsey Porter helped me with initial encouragement, smiling confidence, and competence.

For the San Francisco Public Library's extensive resources, I am particularly thankful.

Introduction

Yeah, too many awful bad guys, but that's what the news likes to talk about.

—STEVE GIORDANO

What really grabs at the vitals, juices a species that moves deftly on two feet with useful opposable thumbs and largish calculating brains, are the impure types, the criminals, the villains, and even run-of-the-mill bad guys.

California has had its share—perhaps more than its share—of bad guys who were hated by their contemporaries for well-publicized bad deeds. Many bad guys were also "jerks," guilty of a more nuanced badness in the court of public opinion—treating others badly, often horribly. Bad guy jerks make it tough on others, on society, the law, moral standards, and they cause harm and throw away the comforting balance of life.

Given an inspiring tale or a there-but-for-the-grace-of-a-deity-go-I tale of wrongdoing, the bad guys' conniving and deeds win our lurid interest. Few Homo sapiens will ever be heroic, be saintly, or perform a miracle. Heroes get medals, saints stand on pedestals, and even miracle workers are elevated to superhuman status. Admirable as they are, most of us will never be a hero, a saint, or a miracle performer.

Why, then, is a sinner's story more seductive than an angel's? There's the horror of ending up as bad as the villain. There's the quandary of causing physical or mental distress or both by action or inaction. There's a relieved righteousness at an evil path not taken. Motives are suspect, and we like that mystery, not knowing everything about everyone instantly, having to ferret it out, even in today's easy-access information age.

Jerk behavior hooks us with snatches of clues, touches of malice, mayhem, disorder, criminal intent, or crazed violence. Jerks are irritating, malicious, and disgusting. The violence can be terrifying.

California Supreme Court Justice David S. Terry fought duels with sometime friends and picked fights with enemies, a violent streak in a powerful man that ultimately led to his shooting by a United States Supreme Court Justice's bodyguard.

Jerks—now or in the past—may be more than an isolated individual, as in the case of Ku Klux Klan members who "invaded" a city council with a 1924 takeover, or San Francisco vigilantes who took the law into their own hands, without trial, meting out capital punishment by hanging. There are situational jerks, such as a group that conspires to do dastardly deeds against others, usually for profit: organized crime syndicates and Wall Street financiers ushering in the Great Recession leap to mind. Or, on a more individual basis, Bernard Madoff set up an elaborate Ponzi scheme situation to dupe investors with lucrative promises of enormous payouts.

"Those who do not remember the past are condemned to repeat it," wrote philosopher and writer George Santayana in *Life of Reason, Reason in Common Sense* in 1905. The adage is usually adjusted to "those who do not know history are doomed to repeat it."

It's not hard to find examples of "jerks" in California's history. Racism is rampant against Native Americans, including the Modocs of far northern California, in Dennis Kearney's virulent campaign against the Chinese, and in discrimination and violence against Mexicans and Mexican-Americans, from the time of bandido Tiburcio Vásquez in the nineteenth century to twentieth century campaigns by the Ku Klux Klan in Southern California. Political corruption flourished from at least the California Gold Rush in 1848 on, exemplified by San Francisco political operative Abe Ruef in the era before the 1906 Earthquake and Los-Angeles–based oilman Edward Doheny's involvement in the Teapot Dome Scandal. Even 1950s movie industry blacklisting had a precedent in Roscoe "Fatty" Arbuckle's 1920s blacklisting—though with anti-Communist as opposed to morality-policing motives.

Yet, few bad guys or jerks are *all bad*. Most of the California jerks profiled in this book have other dimensions to their deeds, backgrounds, or personalities. The pirate who torched Monterey in 1818 is anything but a pirate to Argentineans: Hipólito Bouchard is a national hero. Civil engineer William Mulholland's water policies in Southern California had dire effects for outlying communities and a 1928 dam collapse resulted in a deadly outcome, but his Department of Water & Power provided water to Los Angeles and its booming population. These two jerks who frame the California history in this book are riveting because of their multiple dimensions and the eras in which they lived and worked.

It's easy to condemn rackets in San Francisco's Chinatown commanded by "Little Pete," or stagecoach robber "Black Bart," but each was a product of his time, culture, and economics. They and the other "jerks" in this book exploited what was available to make a living—and a reputation. The legendary Robin Hood character in England's Sherwood Forest is revered in modern times for cocky and earnest swashbuckling, but "take from the rich and give to the poor" is logical only in the context of a country close to bankruptcy from funding its sovereign's Crusades campaign. Hood the Robber would have been violating the law. Each "jerk" operates only in the context of his own time, influences, and events.

Of all the United States, California has always been considered different, on the edge of the continent, restless and churning. The state with the largest population—more than thirty-seven million residents at the 2010 US Census—started its recorded history with the settlement of Alta (Upper) California, a backwater province of Mexico in a remote section of the eighteenth-century Spanish Empire. Imposing Christian conversion on Native American groups they encountered, Franciscan padres built twenty-one mission church-factory complexes up the California coast, from San Diego, Santa Barbara, and Carmel (near Monterey) to San Francisco and beyond. A tandem military presence was housed in presidios with sparse emigrant settlements nearby.

By the early nineteenth century, the Spanish crown's power and influence were waning, and those living in backwater settlements were restless. The Upper California settlements, primarily a land grant cattle and sheep ranching culture producing hides and tallow for Spain, were largely left alone. This *californio* culture of wealthy local ranchers, fiestas, *vaqueros* (cowboys), and independence was later idealized as a rosy and bucolic time.

The missions were beginning to decline. Enclaves like the major Spanish settlement at Monterey were vulnerable. Hippolyte de Bouchard sailed up, attacked and burned part of Monterey in 1818.

In 1821, Mexico gained independence from Spain. The rancho land grant culture continued, with more Mexican settlers and Mexican influence. Americans seeking land and commercial opportunities arrived, too, some by wagon train, some by ship. During the Mexican American War from 1846 to 1848, Americans openly promoted independence from Mexico and annexation by the United States. In February 1848, the United States gained vast territory from Mexico under the favorable terms of the Treaty of Guadalupe Hidalgo.

The month before, in January 1848, John Marshall had discovered gold at John Sutter's mill in Coloma. News travelled and the California Gold Rush to the Sierra Nevada foothills was on. With vast numbers of prospectors and opportunists pouring in through San Francisco and on to Sacramento's proximity to the ore and gold-yielding streams, the real fortunes were to be made in providing prospecting materials and the mercantile necessities for daily life. Four Sacramento merchant entrepreneurs parlayed their profits into a shaky enterprise that ultimately became the western stretch of the Transcontinental Railroad in 1869.

Frontier justice was meted out in San Francisco and in the mother lode gold rush country in the 1850s by mobs who decided who had committed a crime and who should be immediately lynched or hanged. Chinese arriving in the gold fields were allowed to sort through the white miners' leavings (tailings) and soon banded together in Chinatowns for self-protection. Prohibited from bringing families to California, the men worked hard and earned the envy of others—including workers incited to violence by labor activist Dennis Kearney in San Francisco. Bandidos worked the foothills and central California, giving rise to legends of ruthless robbers and a Robin Hood take-off, El Zorro, savior of the poor and oppressed.

Graft and corruption were rampant, exemplified by the corrupt regime of San Francisco Mayor Eugene Schmitz and his political henchman, Boss Abe Ruef, in 1906. Twentieth century woes ranged from leftist labor strife before the US entry into World War I, where a labor leader was framed for a bombing he didn't order or carry out; enmeshment in the Teapot Dome oil scandal; persecution of a film star as an excuse to implement a public morals code; secret Ku Klux Klan infiltration of city politics; and a dam disaster that should have been averted.

Historic bad guys weren't absent in California in the 1930s Depression; during and after World War II; during the Cold War, 1960s assassinations, racial riots, and anti-Vietnam War demonstrations; nor have they been absent for more recent venal graft, corruption, and terror that are beyond this book's timeline. All have echoes in earlier California history whose bad guys and jerks can still be examples to disgust, terrify, or warn modern citizens.

Not all jerks and bad guys are criminals, since not all are tried or even guilty of criminal behavior. Yet, the badness or evil they commit can make their deeds *seem* criminal.

There are other folks whose deeds make them less than criminal jerks because of the circumstances they faced. Emigrants crossing the Sierra Nevada in 1846–1847 faced unknown terrain and a record snowfall that resulted in some Donner Party members resorting to cannibalism to survive. Even today, the "Donner Party" evokes an image of humans who went beyond accepted behavior. The moral issues those pioneers faced were and are unsettling. What choice was the right one? Were they jerks?

In these tales of bad guys and jerks, you're invited to see into the motives of some of California's stellar bad apples. Reality bites hard, and it is distasteful, nauseating, bloody to deadly, occasionally poignant, but always riveting.

CHAPTER ONE

Monterey Is Burning:
Hipólito Bouchard Terrorizes Spanish California

Hippolyte de Bouchard—his name changed to Hipólito Bouchard when he became an Argentine citizen—is almost unknown to Californians. Mention California's pirate and there are blank stares.

An official 1819 portrait of Hipólito Bouchard shows a uniformed naval officer, erect and confident, with a slight Mona Lisa–type smile. The right hand reaches for the double row of buttons on his uniform tunic with a stance reminiscent of Napoleon. The eyes under strong, well-shaped brows look to his right, not gazing directly at the viewer or his world. The effect is striking and mysterious. Was this the look of a pirate, as Californians believed, or the knowing look of a privateer under contract to attack the enemies of his adopted country, Argentina?

This ship's captain was a very real threat when he attacked Alta California, outpost of the Spanish Empire that stretched along the California coast from north of San Francisco to San Diego, in 1818. To the inhabitants of Monterey, Santa Barbara, and San Juan Capistrano, his were pirate ships, bent on destruction and plunder. The perpetrator would have denied it vehemently and insisted that he was a privateer. For private voyage backers and the Argentine government, his ships had to turn a profit by seizing whatever they could capture from the hated Spanish enemy.

One country's pirate may be another country's hero. So it is with California's pirate "jerk" who became a hero of the Argentine.

Gobernador Don Pablo Vicente de Solá, governor of Alta California, Spain's least-profitable province, was worried. In fall, this October of the Holy Lord God, 1818, in the capital of Upper Spanish

Oil portrait of naval captain Hipólito Bouchard

California at Monterey, Solá had gotten word from the Santa Barbara Presidio commander: A friendly American sea captain had reported that two pirate ships were under full sail from the Sandwich Islands.

Solá was always writing to His Excellency the Viceroy of New Spain asking for reinforcements for the 410 soldiers he had to defend all of the coast from San Diego to San Francisco. Now, he was worried. If there was an attack by foreign ships, pirates, or naval vessels sailing under some other country's flag, his under-manned defenses were vulnerable.

Governor Solá sent a lookout a few miles north up the coast from headquarters at the Royal Presidio in Monterey to Point Pinos where there was a good vantage point at an overlook. He prayed that the coastal fog that so often rolled over the coastal shrubs and through the pines wouldn't appear and obscure the view.

Solá had the advantage of knowing about the coming threat in advance. Pirates! He started preparations for the defense of the soldiers and settlers in the Royal Presidio compound, the fort called El Castillo that had recently been rebuilt with a better battery, and the warehouse. Franciscan friars and their Indian converts and laborers were a few miles away at Mission San Carlos de Borromeo (Mission Carmel), and they also had to be ready to move. There was an inland cattle ranch that offered a refuge if things became dire.

The governor held office during mounting turmoil in the Spanish Empire that had held sway in most of the Americas for three hundred years. In 1810, insurgents in central Mexico had declared independence from Spain, and their struggle continued. In South America, Simón Bolívar and José de San Martín had rallied the locally born creoles against Spain, working in tandem to push the imperial power out.

Solá, a loyal Spanish officer and citizen, knew of these distant rumblings. Foreign powers, including the new government of Las Provincias Unidas del Rio de la Plata, also known as Argentina, were aggressive and particularly eager to have revenge on the old oppressor, Spain.

If pirates were on the way, well, in these waters pirates were likely to be privateers. The French called them corsairs. It seemed a legal technicality when an attack was imminent, but pirate or privateer, any vessel that wasn't flying the flag of Spain was not officially welcome.

Starting in the sixteenth century, European and emerging powers like Argentina issued an official document called a *lettre de marque* or *lettre de course* to private ship captains who were known as corsairs or privateers. They were authorized to fight enemies, capture enemy treasure, and provide voyage investors and the government with portions of captured valuables. Unlike the national navies, corsairs took the risks and cost the governments nothing. Privateer captains and crews retained a portion of captured treasure for services rendered, their profit.

Most privateers, including England's Francis Drake, also had a patriotic mission: to raise a flag in the name of their government. Unlike the cinematic portrayals of pirate bad guys like Peter Pan's nemesis, Captain Cook, or not-quite-all-there Captain Jack Sparrow in *The Pirates of the Caribbean,* real pirates and licensed privateers were master seamen, navigators, warriors, and strategists, out to make their living and reputation, but always with an eye on the next lucrative voyage.

Solá knew that Alta California received unofficial visits from American and British ships, and there was even some very illegal but necessary trading with the detestable Russians who had very profitable settlements not far north of San Francisco's Presidio. Pirates or privateers, two ships sailing together at top speed for the coast with bad intentions, now that was trouble.

Privateer Hipólito Bouchard was heading toward California after rancorous disputes with King Kamehameha in the Sandwich—later Hawaiian—Islands. In defiance of the instructions under which the Argentine government had issued the privateering letter to his underwriter, Bouchard had embarked on a round-the-world voyage in July 1817. His mission was to attack and take as a prize any other ship's cargo that belonged to Spain, or, if that wasn't possible, to destroy Spanish ships and cargo.

Hippolyte de Bouchard, born in Southern France in 1780, grew up in a country undergoing upheaval and revolution. The sea and Napoleon's navy offered opportunity for a young man. He served in campaigns in Egypt and Haiti. The American and French Revolutions had sparked independence movements in the New World directed against the Spanish Empire. Nowhere was the desire to throw off colonial rule stronger than in South America. The United Provinces of the Silver River, Argentina, had succeeded in 1816.

Bouchard had arrived in Buenos Aires in about 1810, married well, and become an Argentine citizen, taking the Spanish first name Hipólito. He was a volatile, perhaps ruthless, captain when he commanded a privateer ship to disrupt Spanish commerce along South America's Pacific Coast. Life on a ship was tedious, and food was limited and monotonous. Often the food was spoiled. When on land or in a port, the food might not be much better. Rats were everywhere, and below decks were rank. The weather and seas were hazardous, too. Discipline on the high seas was strictly enforced. Although the crew had to obey every instruction, when it came to taking prize ships or trading prisoners, the crew—with a vested interest in the voyage's profits—had some say.

Bouchard was in command of the 464-ton frigate *La Argentina*. Most of his officers had also arrived in Argentina from Europe and England. In 1817, the privateer sailed east from Buenos Aires to Madagascar and helped a British captain prevent slave traders from embarking victims. When half his crew got scurvy, he ordered them buried in sand up to their necks and lost forty men; forty-four survived the "cure." Near Borneo, local pirates on small outrigger boats attacked the frigate. Bouchard watched one captain jump into the sea to his death, kept some of the Malays as crewmen, and then sunk some other pirates on their own ship.

He blockaded the important Spanish trade-port, Manila, for two months without taking any ships or cargoes; that trade had dried up with Mexico's revolt against Spain. Another time, a captured brigantine and schooner disappeared within a few days, perhaps making for a safe port. An attempt to take Manila-Canton trading ships failed in bad weather.

Bouchard was desperate, his sailors sick, and the stock of food depleted. There was no prize yet to pay for the voyage and make it profitable. *La Argentina* sailed for the Sandwich Islands. It was mid-August and the islands would have been ideal for crew health, rest, and relaxation. But Bouchard learned that King Kamehameha had bought an Argentine 280-ton corvette, the *Santa Rosa de Chacabuco,* from mutineers. Demands that the king give up the ship and the mutinous crew were rebuffed. Finally, Bouchard paid for the ship, got the mutineers returned—except for one who Bouchard thought the king had permitted to escape. Threatened with bombardment by *La Argentina,* the Hawaiian king turned the man over. Bouchard had the offender executed and the rest of the mutineers lashed with whips.

Peter Corney, an English ship's lieutenant in the fur trade, met Bouchard during *La Argentina*'s Hawaii stay. Corney described Monterey in Spanish Alta California where he had been in 1815, its lack of military defenders, and the accessible coastal landscape. Who knew what the warehouse treasure house might hold or what other Spanish riches or ships there might be close to Monterey's fine harbor? It was known that Spain wasn't sending more troops or money to pay the soldiers who already served there, and that the supply ships from coastal Mexico had been disrupted by all the privateers' activity against Spain. The Alta California province was pretty much on its own. Were Alta California officials hoarding all the wealth for themselves?

Bouchard, intrigued, made Corney the captain of the *Santa Rosa,* and they sailed east in late October 1818. The captains agreed: There was to be an assault on Monterey, Alta California's capital, and the crews and ships must be ready.

Twenty-seven days later, on November 20, the skies were clear when the black-hulled *La Argentina* and the *Santa Rosa* were sighted by the man posted at Point Pinos. Bouchard and Corney expected to make a surprise assault. But Governor Solá's plan was in place. Mounted soldiers, militiamen, and artillerymen gathered at the curved wall gun battery. Forty men waited.

Suddenly, there was no more wind to fill the privateer ships' sails. Five miles from shore and within sight of the coast, they were too close and too desperate not to try to get to the shore. Rowboats were put overboard and *La Argentina* was pulled three miles toward the harbor where she dropped anchor. Meanwhile, later that night, Corney had positioned the *Santa Rosa* one-quarter mile from shore. The Spanish demanded to see his ship's papers. Corney replied in English. The Spanish finally understood that papers would be presented in the morning. Quietly, Bouchard ordered his sailors into boats to attack the battery under cover of darkness, but his orders weren't obeyed. The men who had rowed to tow *La Argentina* may have been too tired.

As dawn came on November 21, Spanish preparations ashore were evident. Somehow, the Spanish had known that the arriving ships were hostile. Corney decided to act. He quickly ordered Argentina's flag raised on the *Santa Rosa* and commenced firing his cannons up the El Castillo fort's defensive wall. The defenders' cannons—and perhaps an additional battery on the beach—fired back, aiming low at the corvette in the water. Seven rounds were fired before the *Santa Rosa* sailors hauled down the Argentine flag, got out the rowboats, and dashed across to Bouchard two miles out on *La Argentina*.

Bouchard had seen it all. So far, Bouchard, the privateer-pirate (whose privateer commission had already expired!) had failed. The first battle was won by the shore battery, and no Spaniard had been killed.

Solá demanded that the corvette captain come ashore. Instead, an American officer, Joseph Chapman, and two sailors rowed to shore. Solá was disgusted with their excuses and took them prisoner. The governor would have liked to seize the *Santa Rosa* or fire cannonballs into the ship and sink it, but he had few men and wanted to conserve ammunition.

Whatever Bouchard thought of the initial skirmish, it was time to be brazen. He quickly prepared a written demand for the surrender of Alta California, and had it rowed ashore. Governor Solá replied that the ships would be repelled and his loyal Spanish citizens would fight to the last drop of blood. He offered to send the *Santa Rosa* back out to *La Argentina* and Bouchard if the privateer paid for the service. There was no reply.

In the darkness that night, Bouchard's boats got uninjured battle survivors off the *Santa Rosa*. It was time for another bold move.

In the morning, armed with muskets, spears, and a few small cannons, Bouchard, his officers, and 187 men rowed to shore in small boats. Bouchard had decided on a land attack on the El Castillo fort, and the men marched along the shore near modern-day Cannery Row. Governor Solá had ordered everyone out of the fort and to the Presidio. Bouchard's force took the fort without a fight, and the Spanish flag was quickly lowered.

The next target was the Presidio, where the defense troops, their families, the governor, military commanders, mission padres, and others lived in adobe structures surrounded by high defensive walls around the perimeter rectangle. Bouchard's troops and cannons traversed the half mile or so to the Presidio. No one present later told the same account of who fired, or if shots were even fired in defense of the Royal Presidio, but Solá had already ordered everyone to evacuate to the rancho. Only one man was at the Presidio when Bouchard arrived, a settler named Molina, who was taken prisoner. The Spanish knew he was a habitual drunk. To the privateers, he was an enemy captive, a potential bargaining chip.

From November 22, the flag of Las Provincias Unidas del Rio de la Plata flew over the Royal Presidio at Monterey. For the moment, the province technically, if not physically, belonged to Argentina.

Whether serving with a privateer or with a pirate whose privateer's license had expired, the crewmen still needed to make a profit. Surely the deserted Presidio *must* have treasure? Food and clothing were commandeered for personal use; everything was torn apart to send provisions back to Bouchard's ship. Animals were shot and left, actions Solá attributed to rebel rage at not finding soldiers to shoot or valuables. The San Carlos Cathedral inside the Presidio and Mission Carmel were not touched, salvation later attributed to Bouchard's policy forbidding destruction of church property.

Troops arrived at the rancho refuge from San Francisco and San Jose. Monterey's defenders kept track of the Presidio pillage from afar. Bouchard sent another demand to Solá, that Chapman and the two sailors be returned within three days or the Presidio would burn.

Three days later, most of what could burn at the Presidio was torched, but not the cathedral church. Adobe mud homes' wooden beams burned, the barracks went up in smoke, and furniture and personal belongings were a loss. There was nothing left to claim or pillage, so Bouchard took two cannons for the *Santa Rosa* that was being repaired for the voyage south. On November 27, *La Argentina* and the *Santa Rosa* sailed away.

Monterey had been attacked by pirates! The raiders had acted like pirates, hadn't they? Not admitting who they were. Firing the corvette's cannons. Demanding surrender. Landing without leave from the governor. Marching up to the Castillo battery, then taking the Presidio, pillaging everything, shooting the animals, and putting the Royal Presidio to the torch. Governor Solá quickly got Monterey residents busy inventorying the losses and starting to rebuild.

But, if the pirates were sailing south, what was next for Alta California? Solá's scouts reported the pirates' landfall December 4 at the relatively remote Rancho del Refugio north of Santa Barbara. Bouchard expected to find Spaniards who had tortured Mexican independence sympathizers, or, more likely, smuggled goods and coins. Sixty men disembarked, found no one at the rancho, and then started tearing things apart looking for valuables. An officer and two sailors were seized by Spanish horsemen, infuriating Bouchard who burned all the buildings.

To get the men back, they sailed twenty miles south to Santa Barbara where there was another presidio. Bouchard's progress along the coast was paralleled on land by mounted Spanish horsemen. On December 8, Bouchard offered a flag of truce and asked the presidio commander for a prisoner exchange, three crewmen for Molina. Done, agreed presidio commander Don José de la Guerra y Noriega, avoiding Argentine flag-raising, plundering, or torching of Santa Barbara. Bouchard's men took their shipmates and departed after promising to not land anywhere else in Alta California.

Bouchard had lied. Faced with a long voyage down the coast to Baja California and beyond, he needed provisions. The ships anchored in a small bay on December 16. A small town and its mission, San Juan Capistrano, were visible inland. Bouchard offered another trade: Send me provisions and I'll spare the town. The reply insultingly offered powder and shot. Again incensed, Bouchard ordered Corney to land armed men and small cannons and to occupy and plunder the now-deserted town. Corney's troops broke into the wine and an inebriated pillage ensued, with drunken soldiers, Corney remembered later, lashed to field pieces for the return haul to the ships.

What had Bouchard accomplished in a month of privateering along California's coast? He'd burned a provincial capital at the distant end of a crumbling empire and a smuggler-insurgent sympathizer's ranch. He'd traded one useless drunkard for three men who'd been taken prisoner. Bouchard's cohort had plundered food, clothing, wine, spirits, and badly needed supplies, but there had been no treasure, no gold, silver, jewelry, or other valuables.

Argentina's flag had briefly flown over California. Inhabitants of the remote land claimed to have been bombarded, invaded, and sacked, yet Solá and his citizenry had out-maneuvered a pirate who hated them because they were Spanish. Soon, in 1821, the rebels that Bouchard supported in Mexico would win their independence from Spain. Alta California would belong to Mexico, and Don Pablo Vicente de Solá would briefly serve as Alta California's first Mexican governor.

Bouchard's fate was to finally capture some ships and burn others to the water on his way home. Arriving in Valparaiso, Chile, it was discovered that he sailed with an expired privateering document, and, by implication, was a pirate. One of his seized ships was Danish and should not have been a target. Reports of other illegal seizures during the voyage surfaced. Bouchard threatened authorities and was imprisoned. The court set up to decide vessel ownership and piracy exonerated Bouchard, but the voyage had not made enough to cover costs.

Bouchard's checkered and occasionally heroic career continued as he entered the service of Peru and served briefly as the Peruvian fleet's vice admiral. For his services to Peru, he was given ranchland where his vineyards' production was used for brandy. Bouchard died in his sixties in relative obscurity. More than a century later, Argentina honored Bouchard as a hero of the war of liberation and independence—a privateer in the service of his country.

Sources

The City of Monterey claims California's pirate as its own, although other areas south of Monterey also claim depredations by Bouchard's men. Dennis Copeland, a historian and archivist for the City of Monterey, recommends Peter Uhrowczik's *The Burning of Monterey: The 1818 Attack on California by the Privateer Bouchard* (Los Gatos, Calif.: Cyril Books, 2001), as the most accurate and informed account of the Bouchard forces' attack on Monterey. Uhrowczik, who accessed primary source documents in Argentina, includes translations of reports by Bouchard and Solá to their superiors, detailing events of Bouchard's "visit." The succinct narrative, filled with facts about the events, is readable and not biased for or against Bouchard or Solá.

The terror of real people under attack by pirates is poignantly narrated by the fictional son of a Spanish fisherman who is captured by Bouchard's crew in the young adult novel by Kristiana Gregory, *The Stowaway: A Tale of California Pirates* (New York:

Scholastic, Inc., 1995). Bouchard's name is barely mentioned in California's early history, and there is not much about his brave and brazen circumnavigation of the globe for Argentina from 1817–1818. Yet, there is endless material about pirates and privateers, much of it speculative or romantic. For a visually rich and evocative primer on the "Robbers of the Seas," there is *Eyewitness Pirate* (New York: DK Publishing, revised edition 2007), written by Richard Platt and photographed by Tina Chambers.

CHAPTER 2

Survival in the Sierra
The Donner Party Eats

Did they or didn't they? Donner Party pioneer-settlers, families trapped in deep Sierra Nevada snows in the winter of 1846–1847, were faced with grim reality: starvation in the mountains. Death seemed imminent. For some who stayed behind in shelters and for others who went off into the endless whiteness, survival meant breaking one of mankind's forbidden taboos: eating the bodies of human beings. Were they jerks?

The rescue parties included some jerks who expected to get paid handsomely for taking survivors out of the mountains. Several rescuers reported to the press that they had found blood and body parts. Their lurid descriptions were stomach-turning. Not all survivors would speak about their experiences. A few records indicate cannibalism occurred, but only one survivor initially talked openly about it.

Almost all of the children who were alive when the party was trapped by snowstorms survived. Many of the adult women survived, too, though fewer men did. One woman's sacrifice to "stand by her man" was unquestionably heroic. Family groups were not always inclined to share with or help other families. Yet, one man without a family made heroic efforts to save others.

This tale of hopeful travelers setting off on an unverified route without benefit of modern day GPS systems, weather forecasts, satellite weather images, and en route webcams—going to ultimate lengths to survive—could have been a heroic story since almost half the party did survive. But, the horror of reported cannibalism lurks forever over the Donner Party's overland-trek-to-California saga. Whether moral reprobates or survivors, in California history, the Donner Party members are usually remembered as the jerks who dined on each other.

Frid 26th Froze hard last night today clear & warm Wind S:E: blowing briskly Marthas jaw swelled with the tooth-ache; hungry times in camp, plenty hides but the folks will not eat them we eat them with a tolerable good apetite. Thanks be to Almighty God. Amen Mrs Murphy said here yesterday that she thought she would commence on Milt. & eat him. I dont that she has done so yet, it is distressing. The Donnos told the California folks that they commence to eat the dead people 4 days ago, if they did not succeed that day or next in finding their cattle then under ten or twelve feet of snow & did not know the spot or near it, I suppose they have done so ere this time.

—Diary of Patrick Breen, Friday, February 26, 1847

Patrick Breen, a devout Irish Catholic, head of the Breen family, and member of the Donner Party, was starving to death in California's mountains. Caught in a succession of nine blizzards that piled snow twenty-two feet high, "Froze hard" was his frequent diary entry. He and the others had been mostly eating boiled ox hides since early November.

An alluring trail shortcut that was anything but short, poor timing, and the harshest winter in recorded California history, had dovetailed into disaster for the Donner Party emigrants. Death, frostbite, cold, sickness, and cannibalism were the outcome.

The cover of Lansford W. Hastings's 1845 *Emigrant's Guide to Oregon and California* guidebook touted that it held descriptions of different emigrant routes to Oregon and California. It promised, as most guidebooks still do, "all necessary information relative to the equipment, supplies, and the method of traveling."

A twenty-seven-year-old lawyer, Hastings was an adventurer cashing in on his brief experience guiding one group of wagon train settlers west on the Oregon Trail in 1842. He had tacked on a personal post-trail trip from northwest Oregon down the coast of northern California, then returned to the United States via Mexico and had not been near California's eastern mountains. Hastings's detailed

Emigrant's Guide to Oregon and California was filled with warnings about violent Indians. It contained lists of things emigrants should bring on the westward journey. It mentioned a shortcut.

The lands of the West were beautiful, fertile, and easy to farm, Hastings wrote, and California was an Eden. His descriptions and apparent practical knowledge of terrain and conditions caught the popular imagination. Not revealed in the text was Hastings's ambition to rule a California Republic he would help establish if he could convince enough American settlers—prospective subjects—to move to the Mexican-ruled backwater of California. A trickle of Americans had already arrived in California, mostly by ship around South America or by crossing the Isthmus of Panama. Many had married into *Californio* families with Hispanic heritage, a cattle ranching culture, and comfortable circumstances, or established their own ranchos.

By the 1840s, a desire for land, farms, and an even better life for their children inspired relatively prosperous Easterners to sell successful farms or businesses and venture forth on a months-long journey west along the Oregon Trail. Unlike a modern highway, there were no roads or paths to follow other than the wagon-wheel ruts made by wagons that had passed before. Natural and a few man-incised rock landmarks were known from descriptions and sketches. Where wagon train leaders and groups felt that a detour or shortcut was best for safety or to save time, they might decide to leave the main trail for days or weeks at a time.

Most emigrants took valuables: some gold, silver, jewelry—something to buy food, seeds, homes, and land at the other end. A library and schoolbooks were important signs of civilization, considered vital to setting up in a new life. At the same time, pens, paper, and blank books were packed to document with letters and diaries a unique experience undergone by limited numbers of people. Those who stayed behind would devour accounts of daily life along the trail, details about the weather, landmarks, animals, wagon trains, and scenes of cast-off heirlooms or heavy equipment lying by the trailside to lighten the wagon loads. The emigrants were reporters.

Mountain men had explored the West for decades, with reports of boundless natural resources to be tapped and fertile agricultural valleys. In 1836, newly settled Oregon missionaries Marcus and Narcissa Whitman, who had travelled most of the way by covered wagon, wrote enthusiastic, widely distributed letters home about the new land that excited the imagination.

Economic depressions in 1837 and 1841 contributed to restlessness back East in the United States. A trickle of emigrants started to Oregon in 1841. By 1843, hundreds of wagon companies were moving west. The Oregon Trail gathering point was Independence, Missouri. Wagon trains, oxen, mules, horses, dogs, and outriders first crossed the Missouri River. They travelled 2,170 miles through present-day Kansas, Nebraska, Wyoming, Montana, and Idaho, to Oregon City, Oregon. Some settlers veered off toward southern Oregon.

Others trying to save time getting to the California Eden that Hastings had described started southwest after crossing the Continental Divide. That diversion, the cut-off recommended by Hastings in 1845, required crossing the Wasatch Mountains in Utah, through Great Salt Lake Desert desolation, and beyond to the arid Great Basin. Wagon trains would rejoin the main route to California at the Humboldt River in Nevada. This was the route used by the Donner Party.

The Sierra Nevada range presented a last steep barrier. Mountain summits up to 9,945 feet (at Tioga Pass, the eastern entrance to Yosemite National Park) are common. Mountain throughways are not much lower—6,701 feet at Yuba Pass not far north of the Donner Party route, and 7,239 feet at Donner Summit near where Patrick Breen and his fellow travelers were caught for the winter.

In 1846, the group of emigrants who became the core of the Donner Party wanted to cut time off the California route. Everyone knew that the Stevens-Townsend-Murphy Party had moved its wagons and emigrants across the Sierra Nevada in 1844 with no problems, before winter set in. The core Donner group consulted the *Emigrant's Guide.* Their leaders from Springfield, Illinois, brothers George and Jacob Donner and James Reed, met or corresponded with Hastings. What Hastings didn't admit to in the *Emigrant's Guide,* or to the Donner Party until months later in a note he left along the route, was that it was too late in the year, especially with dwindling supplies, to turn back once the wagons had entered the Great Salt Lake Desert. That omission rates Hastings a spot in the Jerk Hall of Fame.

The Donner wagons included sixty-two-year-old North Carolina–born George and his older brother Jacob, Jacob's wife and seven children and stepchildren, George's forty-four-year-old third wife, Tamsen, and their five children aged less than fourteen years. James F. and Margaret Reed, their four children, including Virginia Reed, and Margaret's ailing mother were fitted out in fine style, in what Virginia called a Pioneer Palace Car. It was two stories high and included a stove and mirror with sleeping quarters arranged on the upper frame. The Donners had two teamsters and an unmarried friend with them; the Reeds had three teamsters, a servant, and a family friend.

Other families joined the Reed-Donner group before it reached the first major stop at Fort Laramie on June 17. Patrick Breen was fifty-one, and his wife, Margaret "Peggy," was forty. They brought along seven children, including one-year-old Isabella (the last Donner Party survivor who died in 1935), and their neighbor, Patrick Dolan.

William Eddy's wife and two children made the journey with him. Eddy survived some of the winter's worst conditions and returned to rescue others. Lavinia Jackson Murphy shepherded seven children, three grandchildren, and two sons-in-law. Franklin and Elizabeth Graves brought nine children, a son-in-law, and a teamster, John Snyder. There were others: the McCutchens and bachelor Charles Stanton, who gave his life to save others. A German, Lewis Keseberg, the only participant to confess to eating human flesh, was accused of killing Tamsen Donner for her money.

Family loyalties were supreme, personalities were strong, and the trail's challenges made Donner Party emigrants cantankerous, physically weak, and hungry. Where had everything gone so wrong?

By 1846, the United States and Mexico were at war. With a published guidebook and a reputation as an emigration and California expert, Hastings had to act if his dream of a republic was to become a reality. He signed on as one leader of an emigrant wagon train organizing to go west in 1846. Hastings advocated taking a shortcut called the Hastings Cut-off, and his suggestion generated lots of excitement. The Donner Party with strong urging from John Reed was tempted to risk the cut-off to carve what Hastings said was 350–400 miles and several weeks off the journey. They would rejoin the main Emigrant Trail to California at the Humboldt River in Nevada. Although Hastings had set out east from California to verify the route in early 1846, information he gave Donner Party leaders later minimized any hardships along the cut-off, and he assured them that he would personally escort the party to California. When Hastings didn't appear, party members found Hastings's notes left on bushes along the way, urging them to continue on with a promise of only a few days' journey ahead.

It was turning into a boom year, the newspapers noted, with seven thousand wagons expected to roll out of Independence, Missouri, in April and May, after the spring rains stopped. The rains continued longer than usual, the wagons' wheels filled with mud, and the starting point was a muddy mess, but the wagons, in preorganized groups, set off.

Few in the Donner group were familiar with rugged mountainous terrain and high-altitude winter snowfall when the Donner and Reed families' wagons rolled out of Independence in mid-May, one of the last groups to depart. They were soon joined by other families. Eighty-seven men, women, children, and infants started out as the Donner Party, with sixty to eighty wagons for sleeping, traveling, and storage of foodstuffs, clothing, furnishings, and heirlooms for the new California homes.

Margaret Reed's mother, Sarah Keyes, died soon after their departure. When the Donner-Reed Party arrived at Fort Laramie on June 27, James Clyman, a mountain man friend who had just seen the cut-off with Hastings on his way east, talked late into the night, warning Reed to ignore the Hastings Cut-off and instead to continue from Fort Bridger on the regular wagon route to California.

By mid-July, the Donnor Party was about halfway to their promised land as emigrants and wagons crossed the Continental Divide. Hastings had sent an open letter to the emigrants, promising to meet them at Fort Bridger if they diverted from the main Oregon Trail/California Trail route. At the Little Sandy River, known as The Parting of the Ways, those bound for California or along the Mormon Trail to Utah went south to Fort Bridger. Hastings had left Fort Bridger by the time the Donner Party arrived, with instructions to follow him on the cut-off. They pulled out on July 31.

A week later, a note from Hastings lying on the brush told them to wait until he returned to lead them. Reed rode out to find Hastings, who only agreed to show Reed the route from a high spot, not to lead the Donner Party himself. Reed returned to try to guide them, wagons, people, and animals, bushwhacking through rough terrain. The Donner Party was already running low on water before the Great Salt Lake was sighted on August 22. By Hastings's party's wagon tracks was another note that they would reach water with two days and two nights of hard desert driving. It wasn't true.

Crossing the salt pan took five days. Oxen fled and there was no water. Those strong and coherent enough inventoried what was left. There was not enough food to return east. Charles Stanton and William McCutchen agreed to ride over the Sierra Nevada to California for help. The Donner Party found the Humboldt River trailhead on September 26. They were back on the California Trail, but early snow had fallen on the mountaintops.

After the weeks of suffering, oxen running off, wagons having to be left behind, and dwindling food supplies, James Reed and teamster John Snyder fought after Snyder beat Reed and his wife, Margaret. Reed pulled a knife and killed the teamster, helped bury him, and then left, banished by the group for the murder.

The Donner Party took a week to rest themselves and their animals for the final 150-mile trek over the Sierra Nevada. They were heading for John Sutter's Fort near modern Sacramento, where Hastings had already arrived with his wagon train party in September. Two years before gold was discovered at his Sutter's Mill in the Sierra Foothills, Swiss trader John Sutter's settlement was the one oasis of civilization and supply post in the area, and Sutter's hospitality was well-known. Banished, James Reed set off immediately and reached California where he begged John Sutter and others for help for the party still toiling along the trail. Winter was coming early and men and materiel were being deployed south for the war effort. Reed could not return to his family.

It got worse for the Donner Party. A Belgian farmer was put out of a wagon and abandoned, and Paiute Indians killed some oxen. Every night got colder. With food on seven mules from John Sutter and two Indians to guide the party, Stanton returned to the Donner Party on October 19. The group ate, rested for five days, and then started along the Truckee River, pushing toward the top of the Sierra Nevada.

On Halloween, George Donner's wagon axle broke at Alder Creek; he sliced his hand trying to repair it. The Donners set up tents. Ahead, five miles on, the other families found a lake (now Donner Lake) below the summit they would have to cross the next day. The first snow fell that night. It was November 1 and the snows were early.

Led by the Indian guides, the group, without the Donner families, tried to get wagons and animals up to the summit. The snow got deeper as they ascended, and the wagons were too heavy. Stanton and one Indian got to the summit and returned for the party. Tired adults and children couldn't make it further and as darkness came, snow fell. By morning, the pass above was snowed in, and the Donner Party—those at Alder Creek and those who returned to the lake shore—were trapped.

The snow fell for eight days, and the families settled in with the two Donner families in separate tents, one with a pine bough and brush extension, and the lake area families in cabins and a brush lean-to against one cabin. Occasionally, someone would go between the Lake Camp and Alder Creek to check with the others and find out news.

Some cattle died, and attempts were made to salvage meat and hides. William Eddy hunted, taking a prairie wolf and an owl, and eventually ducks, a squirrel, and a grizzly bear. It was not enough to feed them. Eddy and others began to kill their cattle.

On November 2, James Reed and McCutchen, with food and horses from John Sutter, set out to rescue those who they knew must have been trapped by snow. They lasted five days before snow made them turn back.

we now have Killed most part of our cattle having to stay here untill next Spring & live on poor beef without bread or salt.
—PATRICK BREEN'S DIARY

November ended with four days and nights of continu-ous snow, and December rushed in with a wild, shrieking storm of wind, sleet and rain, which ceased on the third.
—ELIZA POOR DONNER HOUGHTON,
THE EXPEDITION OF THE DONNER PARTY AND ITS TRAGIC FATE

The weak began to die. Tiny three-year-old Eliza Donner later had her older sisters' memories to remind her:

The little field mice that had crept into camp were caught then and used to ease the pangs of hunger. Also pieces of beef hide were cut into strips, singed, scraped, boiled to the consistency of glue, and swallowed with an effort; for no degree of hunger could make the saltless, sticky substance palatable. Marrowless bones which had already been boiled and scraped, were now burned and eaten, even the bark and twigs of pine were chewed in the vain effort to soothe the gnawing which made one cry for bread and meat.

There were several November attempts by the sixteen to twenty strongest adults to get out, but deep snow and more bad weather turned them back.

Monday 30ᵗʰ Snowing fast wind W about 4 or 5 feet deep, no drifts, looks as likely to continue as when it commenced no living thing without wings can get about
　　　　　　　　—PATRICK BREEN'S DIARY, NOVEMBER 30, 1846

On December 16, fourteen people, including the two Indians from Sutter's Fort and one teenager, strapped on snowshoes constructed by Franklin Graves, the only one familiar with moving through deep snow, and left the lake. The farewells were tearful, but husbands and wives, sons and daughters, promised to return after they trekked 150 miles to Sutter's Fort or Fort Sacramento for help. The Snowshoe Party called itself the Forlorn Hope and looked to Stanton and the Indians as guides.

They each carried eight pounds of beef. They had no shelter. They made it to the summit and pass and crossed. Several days along, Stanton became snow-blind and had trouble reaching the camp. He was last seen sitting by a campfire smoking his pipe.

It started raining, then snowing hard on December 21 for three days. Some snowshoers became delirious. On the 24th, they couldn't light a fire, so William Eddy got them all together intertwined under blankets and let the snow cover the blankets as insulation. There was discussion of a return to the lake cabins, retracing their footsteps. Only Eddy and the women were determined to move on. Patrick Dolan proposed that they should cast lots to see who would die so that the others could have the body to eat. Finally, they agreed to go on until someone died. Eventually, deprivation, cold, and starvation started killing the party off, including Dolan.

In February 1847, John Sinclair, alcade (administrator-judge) of California, recorded Eddy's and other survivors' statements:

On the twenty-seventh they took the flesh from the bodies of the dead; and on that, and the two following days they remained in camp drying the meat, and preparing to pursue their journey.

They had named the place The Camp of Death. On December 31, they saw the Sacramento Valley. Next was a scrabble up canyon walls, swollen and bleeding feet, and eating the hide bindings of the snowshoes. The companions' dried body meat was exhausted and someone proposed killing the Indians. Eddy warned them to flee. When Jay Fosdick died on January 6, the others, except Mrs. Fosdick, ate the meat. On the 8th, the survivors were arguing about killing each other. The next day, they found one of the Indians dead and the other dying. Their flesh was eaten, too. By January 10, they had found an Indian trail, and two days later came to an Indian settlement. On January 17, two men and five women, the Snowshoe Party survivors, were brought to Johnson's Rancho. They had made it to California in a month, eating the flesh of those who died along the way. The news quickly reached San Francisco that sixty emigrants were still snowed in, in dire straits in the mountains.

Back at the cabins, people were starting to die. On January 4, a group of four or more, including twelve-year-old Virginia Reed, set out to cross the mountains. It was cold, and they stopped for a day to make snowshoes. Finally, on January 7, with no path in sight, they returned to the cabins.

that same night thaere was the worst storme we had that winter & if we had not come back that night we would never got back
    —Virginia Reed, letter to her cousin Mary Keyes, May 16, 1847

Conditions deteriorated further. At the end of January, the Graves family took the hides that the Reeds had left to eat as a payment for money due. Fifteen-year-old Landrum Murphy starved to death in front of his family.

The seven men of the First Relief Party left Johnson's Rancho in early February. James Reed got military backing and support from Yerba Buena (soon to be San Francisco) residents, and left the coast on February 8 to be part of the Second Relief company. In the mountains, those who could still walk pulled corpses from the cabins out to the snow and attempted burial.

The First Relief reached them on February 19, and one of the women crawled out of a hole in the snow when they yelled. Daniel Rhoads later wrote, "They had been living on dead bodies for weeks." Jacob Donner had died and George Donner's hand was infected. The relief gave what they could, guarded their equipment from theft, and on February 22, left with twenty-one "strong ones we chose as we couldn't get the weak ones across" explained Riley Moutry to *The Santa Cruz Sentinel* decades later.

Patrick Breen, still at the lake camp, was distressed by Mrs. Murphy's comment that she would commence on Milt and eat him, and noted it in his February 26 diary entry. The First and Second Rescue parties met, and James Reed saw his wife, Margaret, and two of their children. The Second Relief found the survivors even weaker, with bare bones and half-eaten bodies of those who had starved to death. Jacob Donner's widow was ill, and George Donner was "helpless." Reed noted that Tamsen Donner, relatively robust, would not leave George. Seventeen survivors, including the two remaining Reed children, and the nine Breens, including Patrick, left with the Second Relief in early March. William Eddy and William Foster, a Murphy son-in-law, arrived with the Third Relief party soon after to find that their children had died. They rescued four children, including three Donners and a sixteen-year-old brought along as a handyman. When salvage parties arrived at the lake in April, they found thirty-two-year old Lewis Keseberg alive and, it was said, human flesh nearby.

Forty-six Donner Party members survived, including the Reeds and Breens. Were they cannibals? Did they eat the flesh of fellow human beings? A few admitted to it, most did not.

I have not wrote you half the trouble we have had but I have wrote enough to let you know that you don't know what trouble is. But thank God we have all got through and the only family that did not eat human flesh. We have everything but I don't care for that. We have got through with our lives but Don't let this letter dishearten anybody. Never take no cutoffs and hurry along as fast as you can.

—DONNER PARTY SURVIVOR, TWELVE-YEAR-OLD VIRGINIA REED, LETTER TO HER COUSIN MARY KEYES, MAY 16, 1847

SOURCES

Lansford W. Hastings's *The Emigrant's Guide to Oregon and California,* published in 1845 by George Conclin in Cincinnati, was the guidebook that promoted California's qualities and ease of access and is credited, along with a meeting with Hastings, with the Donner Party's decision to take their wagon trains over the High Sierra route. The complete text is in the Brigham Young University, Harold B. Lee Library Special Collections, Provo, Utah, and online at contentdm.lib.byu.edu/cdm4/document.php?CISOROOT=/TrailGuides&CISOPTR=2978.

The National Park Service Oregon National Historic Trail site, at nps.gov/oreg, covers the route, history, and trials of the Great Migration.

In 1996, self-described amateur historian Daniel M. Rosen compiled Donner Party members' day-by-day diary entries, letters home, post-rescue accounts, and some newspapers' coverage for the 150th anniversary of the trek for his website at www.donnerpartydiary.com. With a minimum of commentary, Rosen places concurrent narratives in the same time line, so that readers follow what was happening on any date at the Lake Cabins, with the Snowshoe Party, and Rescue Parties' attempts.

In September, 1911, Eliza Poor Donner Houghton, a Donner Party survivor who was three years old in winter 1846–1847, published a long memoir based on her family members' memories, research, and interviews by historian C. F. McGlashan. She blames

Keseburg for her mother's death, then, with McGlashan's detective work, is able to meet him and accepts his statement to her that he was not a murderer. *The Expedition of the Donner Party and Its Tragic Fate* can be read as a Project Gutenberg e-book at http://gutenberg.net/1/1/1/4/11146/ where, "This eBook is for use of anyone anywhere at no cost and with almost no restrictions whatsoever. You may copy it, give it away or reuse it under the terms of the Project Gutenberg license included with this eBook or online at www.gutenberg.net."

Ken Burns wrote, directed, and co-produced *The Donner Party* for the American Experience, a production of PBS/WGBH Educational Foundation, available online with the video's transcript and related materials at pbs.org/wgbh/americanexperience/films/donner.

In 1960, George R. Stewart revised his 1936 book, *Ordeal by Hunger: The Story of the Donner Party* (Houghton Mifflin Company, Boston), to reflect more current information. His compilation of the motivations for the movement west and a narrative that evokes Eddy seeing mirages, for example, gives the story an individual's personality. More recently, in 2008, Ethan Rarick's *Desperate Passage: The Donner Party's Perilous Journey West* (New York, Oxford University Press) took Tamzene (the spelling he uses) Donner, Patrick Breen, Margaret Reed, and others at the beginning of each chapter to react to what happened on the trail and at Donner Lake.

Donner Memorial State Park, parks.ca.gov, preserves what is left of the cabins and cabin sites, at what quickly became known as Donner Lake. Modern winter visitors can snowshoe, cross-country ski, or hike around. The year-round recreational area near Interstate 80 includes the Pioneer Monument near the Murphy Cabin site that is dedicated to 1840s emigrants and rises twenty-two feet to show how high the snows were in 1846–1847. The Emigrant Trail Museum includes the Donner Party story. Despite the tendency for deep snow here, years later, Southern Pacific Railroad engineer Theodore Judah suggested that the Transcontinental Railroad track should run over Donner Pass.

CHAPTER 3

String 'Em Up
San Francisco Vigilantes Execute Frontier Justice

San Francisco politics were in turmoil once 49ers began pouring into the quiet bayside backwater. So was the legal system. No authority could really control the thousands of determined prospectors and other arrivals seeking to exploit the rumored riches coming from the Sierra Nevada foothills. Lawlessness that existed in gold country led to fights, massacres, duels, lynchings, and vigilantism, where locals were likely to string someone up before the law determined if the man or woman was a criminal.

That type of summary justice existed in San Francisco for two brief incarnations as a Committee of Vigilance. It was raw, frontier justice refined by leaders of the committee who acted as hearing officer, trial judge, and final arbiter for anyone who offended the population's sense of justice. Oddly, the vigilante leaders were mostly businessmen trying to protect their interests, not men yelling loudly to whip up mob frenzy. After San Francisco's first go-round in 1851, a Committee of Vigilance, or vigilantes, again took a semblance of law into their own hands in 1856 for three months of fear and terror. That their extra-legal proceedings usually targeted and rid larger society of wrong-doers does not make the vigilantes heroes; using the law for their own ends in the name of the common good makes them jerks.

May God forgive my tormentors.

—JAMES CASEY'S GRAVESTONE INSCRIPTION,
MISSION DOLORES HISTORIC GRAVEYARD, SAN FRANCISCO

William T. Coleman had seen it before in summer 1851. And now, the Monumental Engine Fire Company's bell was again tolling loudly over San Francisco. It was the old summons, the call to vigilance.

Tonight, May 14, 1856, Coleman knew that his hope that there would never again be a need for a Committee of Vigilance had been false. In 1851, it had taken three months for the Committee of Thirteen that people now remembered as the Committee of Vigilance, to arrest and try ninety men. Most of the bad apples got off or were shipped out, and some were turned over to the police and sheriff, but the committee did whip one man and hanged four more.

Coleman had arrived in California with the lure of the Gold Rush in 1849—one of the 49ers. The sleepy village of five hundred souls called San Francisco had thirty thousand residents within a few years, scrambling for a living, a place to live or squat, and competing for every resource. By summer 1851, San Francisco was going from bad to worse. The pursuit of gambling, prostitutes, and dark alley crime became oppressive for those more law-abiding. No man then, or five years later in 1856, went outside without a knife and at least one firearm, a revolver or a pistol. There was murder everywhere, sometimes for no apparent reason. Everyone had a thin skin and took offense at almost any comment as an affront to personal honor.

The newspapers had been full of it in 1851. The *Alta* was bemoaning how bad things were. Arson fires, so dangerous in this wooden city, were ruining businesses. The Sydney Ducks gang, ruthless criminals from Australia, hung around the docks and near Telegraph Hill. After dark, they set arson fires, and then stole whatever was inside the store or business.

Back in 1851, everyone was trying to make California a state and the courts barely functioned. Political office, predictably won by false-bottom ballot box stuffing, was a fiefdom where you could hand your cronies the spoils. Everyone who could get elected made money from bribes.

1856 Committee of Vigilance scaffold awaits a hanging
COURTESY SAN FRANCISCO HISTORY CENTER, SAN FRANCISCO PUBLIC LIBRARY

In June 1851, the brazen John Jenkins—a Sydney Duck—took a safe from a waterside store. Jumping in his getaway boat, he had rowed out into San Francisco Bay. Pursued, Jenkins dumped the evidence, but he was hauled back in.

Volunteer firemen, including the eternal opportunist, Sam Brannan, who had broken the news of the Sutter's Mill gold discovery, were the ones who organized the First Committee of Vigilance on June 9, 1851. The firemen were heroes for fighting the dangerous fires and often had a lot of individual influence in the community and in politics.

One hundred three men, Coleman among them, signed the group's constitution:

> But we are determined that no thief, burglar, incendiary or assassin shall escape punishment, either by the quibbles of the law, the insecurity of prison, the carelessness or corruption of the police, or a laxity of those who pretend to administer justice.
>
> —CONSTITUTION OF THE ASSOCIATION [COMMITTEE OF VIGILANCE]
> JUNE 10, 1851

If the law wouldn't or couldn't do the job, they would be the law. It was the Committee of Vigilance versus the scum of the earth.

One or more members were to be assigned to be in the committee's meeting room twenty-four hours a day to receive any citizen complaints of criminal behavior. Any reports needing a membership decision would call for an assembly and majority vote by those present. If a major crime was charged, the alarm bell—from the Monumental Engine Fire Company—would ring twice every minute. The majority of those responding decided on the verdict and punishment behind closed doors.

After swift committee condemnation, at 2:00 a.m. Jenkins the thief swung for his crime above Portsmouth Square.

A month later on July 11, the Monumental Engine Fire House bell rang the summons again. Englishman James Stuart, a criminal who should have stayed in Australia after he was ordered transported, was reported to have confessed his recent crimes, including murder, to the committee. He was hung from a derrick at the end of the Market Street Wharf.

People started noticing that known criminals must be in terror of the by now seven-hundred-man-strong committee, its instant justice, and public executions. Suspected criminals who didn't voluntarily ship out were heading to the interior, well beyond Sacramento that had its own Vigilance Committee.

Suddenly, in late August, California Governor John McDougall, San Francisco Mayor Charles Brenham, and Sheriff John Hays appeared at committee headquarters and seized committee-condemned criminals Sam Whittaker and Robert McKenzie and confined them in the county jail. The next day, the vigilantes broke into the jail and re-took the two criminals. Fifteen thousand people watched as they were strung up on the committee headquarters building and hanged promptly at 3:00 p.m.

By September 15, the 1851 Committee of Vigilance membership felt that the city had been cleaned up and noted that arson had practically stopped. The Committee of Vigilance voted to disband. Coleman hoped never to hear the bell and never again to sit in sessions to decide sentences for the city's criminal dregs.

But, in 1856, the bell was ringing. After several years with a lower crime rate, the declining economy was making people more desperate. There was less gold coming from the Sierra Nevada foothills. A number of banks with offices on Montgomery Street had had runs on their funds or closed in 1855. Now in 1856, there were fights, murders, and shootings. Low-lifes and ruffians were disturbing San Francisco's peaceful law-abiding citizens, disrupting businesses like Coleman's shipping company, and giving the city a bad name.

In November 1855, an inveterate gambler, Charles Cora, took offense at comments about his mistress and well-known brothel madam, Belle, that had been made by the Northern California district marshal, William H. Richardson. Cora shot Richardson

San Francisco Committee of Vigilance poster
COURTESY SAN FRANCISCO HISTORY CENTER, SAN FRANCISCO PUBLIC LIBRARY

in the street with his derringer and was quickly arrested for the murder and taken to jail. People said it was typical of the lawlessness plaguing the city.

A former banker, James King of William, had gotten friends' backing to start publishing a new newspaper, the *Evening Bulletin,* in October 1855. He named names of those he believed were corrupt politicians and wrote withering editorials pleading for reform.

San Francisco Supervisor James P. Casey, a well-known ballot box stuffer, started his own newspaper, the *Weekly Sunday Times* on Christmas Eve that year. King and Casey quickly engaged in vicious editorial jousting, hurling accusations and insults.

Meanwhile, Charles Cora's trial in January 1856 ended in a hung jury. The jury may have been bribed or swayed by Cora's argument that he was defending his lover, Belle. There would be a second trial.

San Francisco's police department was ineffective, too, San Franciscans charged. No wonder the policemen refusing to do their jobs were suspended! The crime spree seemed to be getting worse.

On May 14, King's editorial scathingly revealed that Casey had once been an inmate of New York's notorious Sing Sing Prison and charged that the supervisor was an expert at ballot box stuffing from his New York days.

Casey wouldn't tolerate the insults and the revelations of his past. He charged into the *Evening Bulletin* office, they argued, and before he left, Casey told King that he would shoot him. Casey told at least one friend and supporter what he planned to do and put his affairs in order. Later that day, near the corner of Montgomery and Washington Streets, Casey shot and wounded King. Supporters got Casey to the safety of a county jail lockup while King was treated by a doctor. The mayor tried to calm the crowds that began to rush to see what had happened.

The Monumental Engine Fire Company bell began to ring the old signal. Going to the assembly, Coleman soon heard what had happened. Committee of Vigilance members, mostly merchants with a vested interest in city affairs and in controlling crime, gathered and elected a new leadership. Coleman was now president of San Francisco's Second Committee of Vigilance.

The reorganized committee wanted Cora, still being held in jail pending a second trial, and Casey, for his attack on the crusading editor. The quick regrouping of the Committee of Vigilance, swelling to 3,600 strong within thirty-six hours of the bell's sounding, had alarmed everyone. On May 16, California Governor J. Neely Johnson, accompanied by Major General William T. Sherman, arrived at the new committee headquarters at 41 Sacramento Street to make a personal appeal to an old friend, Coleman, for the life of Cora and that of Casey—if King should die.

In the streets, the old vigilante militias from 1851 were reforming, too, drilling and marching, riding horses, and readying weapons. Who knew what might be called for? Three hundred armed men guarded the committee building. The seven-hundred-pound Monumental Engine Fire Company bell was brought and mounted on the roof. An armory was set up below the committee meeting rooms and newly designated cells.

The Vigilance Committee ignored the governor's request, and on May 18, it demanded that San Francisco Sheriff David Scanell release both Cora and Casey to committee custody. When the corrupt Scanell who had "bought" his election hesitated to turn Cora over, he was given an hour to reconsider. Casey was taken to committee headquarters. The same hundreds of well-organized vigilantes escorted Cora from the jail one-half hour later.

The committee and the newspapers had regular updates on King's condition. Originally, doctors expected he would recover. The city waited. But the Committee of Vigilance acted.

On May 20, as both Cora and Casey were on "trial" before the committee, news came that King had died at 1:30 p.m. Both men were declared "guilty of murder" on May 21. Three thousand men cleared the streets around the committee headquarters, while platforms to serve as gallows were suspended from the fortress windows. Crowds began to gather, with perhaps twenty thousand people awaiting the execution. At 1:15 p.m. both men emerged. The crowd had heard that Cora had married his Belle. He was silent and calm. Casey told the massed vigilantes and citizens that he wasn't guilty of any crime and that he had never meant to commit murder. Then the cords were cut and the murderers dropped the length of a man.

The vigilantes dispersed until the next summons. The governor was worried about the situation and the Vigilance Committee's defiance. He asked William T. Sherman to meet him and told the major general that he might need to call out the militia. Sherman was California militia commander in San Francisco, but his men would need arms, he explained. On June 3, Governor Johnson called up the militia, declaring San Francisco in a state of insurrection. Together, the men visited the local army commandant and the navy commodore, but both eventually refused to help. It was a local, civilian matter, the army general decided. Sherman resigned his commission in disgust.

The Committee of Vigilance was taking no chances. Not far from the bay, their fortress was barricaded with sand-filled gunny bags that gave the place its nickname, Fort Gunnybags. Roof cannons were extra insurance against government militias.

The next bell summons came on June 21 when California Supreme Court Justice David S. Terry stabbed a Vigilance Committee policeman, the hangman of Cora and Casey, Sterling A. Hopkins, with his Bowie knife. The always volatile Terry was protecting an arms smuggler who was wanted by the committee (see David S. Terry chapter). Terry and the arms smuggler were taken into custody.

Even the police were leaving justice to the committee. On July 24, a gambler, Joseph Hetherington, confronted Dr. Andrew Randall, one of the California Academy of Science founders, in a hotel lobby. Words were exchanged, and both men fired revolvers. Randall slumped down and died the following day. The police took Hetherington into custody but quickly turned him over to the committee.

Justice came quickly, five days later. On a gallows over Davis Street between Fort Gunnybags and Commercial Street, Hetherington and another murderer, Philander Brace, were fitted with nooses and hanged. With each hanging, the crowds outside Fort Gunnybags grew. The Vigilance Committee and its six to nine thousand vigilante supporters still wondered if the militia would arrive and attack their fortress.

Not everyone was hanged. Hopkins didn't die, so Terry wasn't technically guilty of murder. Yet, he had assaulted the committee's own lawman. At the end of Terry's trial on August 7, he was told to resign from his position on the Supreme Court, being unworthy of that office. Fearing a membership backlash, Coleman and his fellow committee officers decided to let Terry "escape" at night through a back door of Fort Gunnybags.

The momentum seemed to be winding down with the summer. The committee had hanged four men. One prisoner, a prizefighter nicknamed Yankee Sullivan, had committed suicide inside Fort

Gunnybags. Twenty-three men were shipped out of San Francisco, two ran away, and two others were known to have fled into the interior of the state. The committee had met in secret, denied their prisoners' rights, and passed judgment without mercy or appeal. The city and evil-doers had learned that violence reaped violent punishment.

It was enough. After a formal parade on August 18, the Committee of Vigilance voluntarily laid down its arms, brought the cannons down from Fort Gunnybags's roof and put away the barricades forever. The heavy bell was returned to the Monumental Engine Fire House across from Portsmouth Square. And William. Coleman went home, sincerely hoping he would never again hear that bell ring twice an hour.

As they controlled the press, they wrote their own history, and the world generally gives them the credit of having purged San Francisco of its rowdies and roughs; but their success has given great stimulus to a dangerous principle, that would at any time justify the mob in seizing all power of government; and who is to say that the Vigilance Committee may not be composed of the worst, instead of the best, elements of a community? Indeed, in San Francisco, as soon as it was demonstrated that the real power had passed from the City Hall to the committee-room, the same set of bailiffs, constables, and rowdies that had infested City Hall were found in the employment of the "Vigilantes."
—The Memoirs of General W. T. Sherman

POSTSCRIPTS

The Second Committee of Vigilance disbanded, but their influence continued as the leaders organized into the People's Party, reformers who were voted into office in the November 1856 election and remained in power for more than ten years.

In 1877, when Dennis Kearney was inciting anti-Chinese sentiment in San Francisco, Committee of Vigilance veteran William T. Coleman again raised a group of followers to fight the violence. This time, they were organized as a Committee of Safety, armed with pickaxes, not guns, and they worked with San Francisco police, not against them.

SOURCES

The Virtual Museum of the City of San Francisco (sfmuseum .org) has participants' written recall of events from Gold Rush and post–Gold Rush history, including contemporary newspaper and tabloid accounts of the Second Committee of Vigilance and memoirs by Lell Hawley Woolley and William T. Sherman. The revised and corrected second edition of *The Memoirs of General W. T. Sherman—Complete* by William T. Sherman (New York: D. Appleton and Company, 1889), can be read as a Project Gutenberg™ e-book at www.gutenberg.net/4/3/6/4361/ where, "This eBook is for use of anyone anywhere at no cost and with almost no restrictions whatsoever. You may copy it, give it away or reuse it under the terms of the Project Gutenberg license included with this eBook or online at www.gutenberg.net." The general, who would become best known for the March across the South and the burning of Atlanta less than a decade later, was in San Francisco to manage a private bank and narrated some of the pivotal 1856 events.

San Francisco Chronicle staff writer and historian Carl Nolte remembers the vigilantes after 150 years in "Recalling the End of the Wild West" (August 18, 2006). In *Murder by the Bay: Historic Homicides in and about the City of San Francisco* (Sanger, Calif.: Quill Driver Books/Word Dancer Press, Inc., 2005), Charles F. Adams includes a chapter, "The Doomed Editor—1856" on the events connecting King, Casey, and Cora. Roger D. McGrath analyzes the vigilantes and other nineteenth-century California violence in his essay, "A Violent Birth: Disorder, Crime and Law

Enforcement, 1849–1890" in *Taming the Elephant: Politics, Government, and Law in Pioneer California,* edited by John F. Burns and Richard Orsi (Berkeley: University of California Press, 2003).

CHAPTER 4

1859 Terry's Terrible Temper
David S. Terry, Bellicose Man of and against the Law

Thin-skinned, trigger-ready, and knife-wielding, one jerk cut a path across California's early state history with his violent temper. Post–Gold Rush San Francisco was made for larger-than-life men of action and resolve. David S. Terry was one of those stand-and-deliver opportunists who came west with the Gold Rush and became a major player in the raw justice and politics of his time. His bad guy career in California included a stabbing, a duel, and an attempted assassination.

After two bouts of vigilantism, in the late 1850s San Francisco was trying to settle down. The United States Congress was discussing slavery and whether a Union of All the People legally and morally trumped states' sovereign rights. There were heated arguments across the nation. Where other leaders used rhetoric and what is today called negative campaigning, Terry, by birth a Southerner and pro-slavery, reacted with violence to what he took as affronts to himself and his beliefs.

Years later during a post–Civil War sojourn in California, an infuriated Terry and the woman who became his second wife attacked one of the country's most respected jurists. In the end, Terry's hotheadedness led to an important legal precedent for strong federal protection of public officials that prevails even today.

David S. Terry
COURTESY SAN FRANCISCO HISTORY CENTER, SAN FRANCISCO PUBLIC LIBRARY

An exaggerated sense of personal honor—a weak mind with choleric passions, intense sectional prejudice, united with great confidence in the use of arms—these sometimes serve to stimulate the instruments which accomplish the deepest and deadliest purposes.
—Edward D. Baker's September 1859 eulogy for his friend,
U.S. Senator David C. Broderick

The famous orator Edward D. Baker, soon to become an eloquent Oregon senator, took less than a half-minute of his lengthy Broderick eulogy to obliquely denounce the volatile personality of David S. Terry. Without mentioning Terry, Baker was describing the man who had fatally shot Broderick three days before. Terry and Broderick had engaged in a duel in the peaceful countryside near Merced Lagoon just across the San Francisco city and county line in San Mateo County.

Any citizen who shall fight a duel, send or accept a challenge, or act as a second or knowingly assist any who should do this shall not be allowed to hold any office or enjoy the right of suffrage.
—California Constitution of 1849, Article XI, Section 2

Things had not gone well for David C. Broderick, challenged to the illegal duel by Terry, his one-time friend. Terry had been elected a California Supreme Court justice in 1855 and had become chief justice in 1857, but he was not re-elected in 1859. Broderick had verbally insulted Terry during the 1859 campaign, and the judge could not ignore the affront. So Terry, the most important legal official in the state, had resigned a few days before the duel.

Terry stood well over six feet, a solid, towering man with gray eyes, a prominent nose, and a beard that began at his lower lip and extended over his bow tie. Born in Kentucky, Terry had moved to Texas at an early age. There he grew up, served with Sam Houston at the Battle of San Jacinto, studied law, was a

Texas Ranger in the Mexican War, ran unsuccessfully for office in Galveston, and then decided to try his luck in the 1849 Gold Rush. Like most other 49ers, he wasn't rewarded by finding gold himself. Instead, he hung out his shingle and prospered while practicing law in Stockton.

With a forceful speaking style, the opinionated Terry left no doubt about his position on any issue. He was never without a Bowie knife in his belt. When he later became a judge, Terry's ever-present Bowie knife was placed in front of him whenever he sat in court.

Men of the era were as violent as the times. Terry was no exception; he quickly became known as a man not to cross lest someone get carved up in a fight.

No one in California could hope to be in politics, the military, or practice or administer law without spending a good amount of time in San Francisco, the state's commercial and cultural universe in the 1850s. The often fractious dealings between racial and ethnic groups and deep convictions over whether men could be enslaved or must be free led most citizens to arm themselves. Add a volatile temper like Terry's, and the fuse was primed to explode.

During the Second Committee of Vigilance's sway in 1856 San Francisco, Terry opposed the vigilantes. On June 21, Justice Terry was with Rube Maloney, a crony of Broderick's who the Vigilance Committee wanted for smuggling arms that were supposedly to be used against the vigilantes. The men weren't friends. But Terry and Maloney, along with several other men who vehemently disagreed with the vigilantes, were in US Navy Agent Dr. H. P. Ashe's office when Committee of Vigilance policeman and recent hangman of Cora and Casey, Sterling A. Hopkins, arrived to arrest Maloney. Faced with drawn guns, Hopkins opted to ask his headquarters at Fort Vigilance to send reinforcements.

Meanwhile, Maloney, Terry, and the others, all armed, decided to walk to their own defensible armory. Hopkins's forces followed. As the Terry-Maloney group approached the Kearny and Clay Streets armory where they would barricade themselves safely inside, Hopkins moved forward to make the arrest while he could.

To deflect him, Terry drew a gun on Hopkins, who tried to get the gun away. In the ruckus, Terry drew his trusty Bowie knife and stabbed Hopkins deep in the left side of the neck.

The Terry-Maloney group immediately fled into their armory and drew bolts across the doors. Word spread quickly, and vigilance men armed with bayonets surrounded the building. After a negotiation with Committee of Vigilance leaders, Terry and Maloney surrendered and were taken to the Committee of Vigilance headquarters at the "fort," where they were locked up. The armory cache, meanwhile, had been quickly hauled away by the vigilantes.

If Hopkins died, said the buzz, then Terry would have *murdered* Hopkins. For that, he could be strung up and hanged, vigilante-style. Many people were bristling for the people's punishment, another corpse swinging above the streets of San Francisco. The crowd, and probably some in the committee leadership, wanted Judge Terry's blood—if only Hopkins would die!

Major General William Tecumseh Sherman had recently resigned his commission and his appointment by California's governor to squelch the Committee of Vigilance. Sherman had heard Terry disparage the committee's leaders, mostly important San Francisco businessmen, as "a set of damned pork merchants."

In the meantime, the bleeding Hopkins had been taken to Fort Vigilance. There, a skilled doctor on duty determined that Terry had slashed the vigilance policeman's larynx, pharynx, and possibly an artery. An operation was performed by candlelight to prevent hemorrhaging. Days later, Hopkins was declared to be on the mend, but Terry's attack still had to be dealt with.

Here was a judge, a state Supreme Court justice, who, if not actually guilty of murder, was then over-ripe for a trial for a vicious assault witnessed by many onlookers. If Terry was convicted of assault, what should his punishment be? The trial in Fort Vigilance went on for five weeks and the panel listened to more than one hundred witnesses' testimony. After two weeks of deliberation, the committee finally ruled that Terry was unworthy of public confidence and should resign his office, a decision considered just too lenient by most vigilantes.

Was this almost-murderer chastened? Did Terry regret his attack on Hopkins?

To avoid bloodshed, the Committee of Vigilance leadership decided to secretly get Terry out of the fort in the middle of the night. The judge quickly took a steamer back to the relative safety of Sacramento, his home, his garden, and his wife, Cornelia, a cousin by marriage. Back in the state capital and unrepentant, Terry returned to his court duties within a few weeks. Maloney had been deported. In August, the Committee of Vigilance voted to disband.

Terry's sights were never far from politics. Both Broderick and Terry had started out as Democrats in the 1840s. By the mid-1850s, white nativists, Southerners, and pro-slavery men had left the Democrat Party and joined the radical Know-Nothing Party. Terry joined, too. The party's unusual name came from secrets known only to members, who, when confronted about their rituals or beliefs, would say they knew nothing about them. The Know-Nothing name changed briefly to the American Party, and Terry was elected to the California Supreme Court on the American Party platform in 1855. By the next year, 1856, the Second Committee of Vigilance had swung into action.

New Yorker David Broderick had also arrived in San Francisco in 1849, poor, self-taught, and well read, the son of an emigrant Irish stonemason who had worked on the US Capitol building. In New York, Broderick had operated a tavern while at the same time swearing off drink, smoking, and gambling at cards himself. Broderick had used his fists in street fights and in barroom brawls, attracting a fiercely loyal gang of friends all too familiar with New York's seamy side. Tammany Hall, impressed by Broderick's heroism as a volunteer fireman, used him to get votes. When he was later ignored by those who were richer and of better background, Broderick had had enough. California looked like a fertile field for a political man. Before he left for California, he told a friend that some day he'd be the senator from California.

Once in San Francisco, Broderick had wasted no time joining and becoming a leader of a volunteer fire department. The high-profile job was crucial in a hastily assembled town of wooden structures where citizens fought fires constantly. Broderick plunged into politics as a Democrat with a rough group of his New York cronies to back him up. The nascent politician needed money. An old friend who had been successful in California suggested that the two of them and another man start a mint to cast five and ten dollar gold pieces. The trio put four and eight dollars' worth of gold into the coins they minted: the rest was "profit." The proceeds gave Broderick funds to further his ambitions against those who would persecute laborers and workingmen, the same men who had sought to make the new state of California a slave state. And California's new constitution outlawed slavery.

The advantage of political office for anyone was power, cemented by the politician's control of appointments to money-making office— the patronage system. By 1851, Broderick was a state senator and became president of the very new California State Senate. Soon, he became the state's acting lieutenant governor when the position became vacant. Broderick lost the 1852 vote by the legislature to be the man in California's vacant US Senate seat. That same year he was injured but not killed in a duel when his watch—and not Broderick's own body—was shattered by a bullet. In 1855, Broderick again lost in a bid to be a senator from California.

Meanwhile, Terry had become the leader of California's pro-slavery forces. One of California's first two senators, William Gwin, owned a Mississippi plantation and slaves. Gwin and fellow elegant-mannered and wealthy Southern aristocrats were known as "The Chivalry." For them, Terry's Southern origins, Texas Ranger reputation, and willingness to proclaim his sentiments made him a vigorous front man to further their cause to make California, or a section of it, a pro-slave state. By 1856, Supreme Court Justice Terry was spoiling to take on the extra-legal Committee of Vigilance. When Terry was held in Fort Vigilance for the attack on Hopkins, Terry felt Broderick did nothing to help him. From that time on, the pro-slavery Terry saw the anti-slavery man Broderick as his enemy.

In 1857, Broderick finally achieved his ambition to be a United States senator. Broderick had supported recently elected President James Buchanan and expected to be handing out California's patronage positions. He thought he had more power than the other senator, Gwin, and the pro-slavery Chivalry movement Gwin was identified with. He hadn't counted on Gwin's friendship with, and the Gwins' lavish entertainment of, the president. As a result, Broderick couldn't get much done in the Senate where Gwin was popular.

As anger between anti-slavery and pro-slavery adherents strengthened, each side verbally assaulted the other. In Congress, the Democrats had become strongly pro-slavery, and a rising Republican Party opposed the institution of slavery. In 1859, Senator Broderick returned to California to personally persuade his Free Soiler faction of the Democrat Party to elect anti-slavery candidates.

Terry addressed a separate convention held by the pro-slavery and Chivalry-backed Lecompton Democrats (who supported a proslavery Kansas constitution adopted in Lecompton, Kansas). Terry had been particularly virulent, describing Broderick's supporters as his ashamed "chattels," who were completely under Broderick's control, effectively calling them Broderick's slaves. Though Terry had played his card attacking Broderick, Terry wasn't renominated to the Supreme Court.

But, Terry's convention address was in the newspapers. Broderick was furious, telling a crowded breakfast dining room gathering at a San Francisco hotel on June 26, 1859, that Broderick had defended Terry in the past against the vigilantes, that Terry had betrayed him, and that Terry was a "damned miserable wretch," adding,

I have hitherto spoken of him [Terry] as an honest man—as the only honest man on the bench of a miserable, corrupt Supreme Court—but now I find I was mistaken. I take it all back. He is just as bad as the others.

It was an insult. Followers of both men urged caution and several notes went back and forth, but in the end, neither man apologized for his comments. Finally, Broderick wrote Terry that it was up to Terry if he judged the language to be offensive. On September 9, Terry's note demanding satisfaction was delivered to Broderick. The duel was on.

They were to use dueling pistols at ten paces, with a count to two. Since losing his first duel where his watch saved him, Broderick had practiced and become a crack shot. The men were well matched as duelists. After a day's delay to throw authorities off their track, Broderick and Terry, their seconds, and Terry's surgeon, were ready on September 13 at the Merced Lagoon. Word had gotten out, and spectators arrived at the chilly spot in the damp morning fog.

The gunsmith prepared Terry's foot-long French pistols that a coin toss had decided would be the weapons, and warned Broderick that his pistol had a hair-trigger that could easily go off. As Broderick, standing with his back to the rising sun shining through the fog raised his pistol on the count of "one," his gun fired the miniature cannonball into the dirt just short of Terry. Terry had also brought his weapon up and fired just as the referee exclaimed, "Two!" Dust seemed to rise from somewhere between Broderick's right shoulder and collarbone, and he slowly collapsed toward the ground, bleeding from the mouth. Someone cried out that it was murder! Terry had been told by his seconds to remain in place. When told that Broderick apparently was badly injured, he said he didn't think so, and "I didn't want to kill him, but to wound him."

The surgeon who was present pronounced Broderick's wound not serious, but he was wrong. The lung had been punctured, and Senator Broderick died three days later. Baker eulogized him. The priest who buried him called Broderick "the most moral of public men." The public and the newspapers screamed for revenge for Broderick's assassination.

After a venue change, Terry was tried in Marin County, north of San Francisco. The verdict delivered by a judge who was Terry's friend was "not guilty," rendered after the main prosecution witness failed to appear when the ferry across San Francisco Bay was delayed.

Terry had gotten away with his part in the duel, but his reputation was tarnished. Terry spent a few years organizing antislavery groups in California where he could, then left for Texas and Virginia by way of Mexico as the US Civil War raged. In Virginia, he was given a commission by the president of the Confederacy, Jefferson Davis, and fought in the two-day 1863 Battle of Chickamauga near Chattanooga. Later, Terry raised his own troops, Terry's Texas Cavalry, a militia that fought late in the Civil War and then adventured in Mexico to try to overthrow the French Emperor Maximilian. For a while, Terry, Cornelia, and several sons tried to make a go of sheep farming in Mexico.

By 1868, Terry was ready to try California again, willing to bear the threats and insults for being a murderer and rebel traitor when he arrived in San Francisco. Back in Stockton, he practiced law and tried to dabble in politics, including an unsuccessful run for California attorney general. Then, his wife, Cornelia, died.

In 1883, his excellent reputation as a lawyer made him an asset when he was retained by Sarah Althea Hill's legal team. Convent-raised, from a good family, and a gorgeous young woman in her twenties, Hill claimed to be the wife of the distinguished former Nevada senator and Comstock Lode banker, millionaire William Sharon. Sharon, in his sixties and living in San Francisco, flatly denied it, filing a federal court suit alleging that a marriage document she had produced was forged and that Hill was trying to blackmail him.

Hill filed for divorce in state superior court, and the judge ruled that the declaration of marriage document was valid and ordered Sharon to pay alimony. Sharon's attorneys appealed in federal court, and after much testimony and wrangling, the decision went against Hill. Hill became known for outbursts in court, threats to shoot or "cowhide" people in the courtroom, and once pulled out a pistol and exclaimed to the judge, "I can hit a four-bit piece nine times out of ten."

US Supreme Court Justice Stephen J. Field had been appointed by Abraham Lincoln to the high court in 1863, after succeeding

Terry as California's Supreme Court chief justice in 1859. Field, who was assigned to oversee California's appellate courts, made summer trips west to hear cases. While taking testimony in Hill's case, Field bluntly ordered that no one was to enter a court of justice armed.

Tho circuit and district court judges ruled that the Hill-Sharon marriage document was a forgery, that Hill could not take advantage of a man whose standing in the community made his testimony truthful—and she could not have trapped him into marriage. Just before the decision, Sharon had died, leaving a will clearly stating that Hill had never been his wife.

Althea, as she was widely known, was furious with the judgment, but she reveled in her personal triumph: She and David Terry were already lovers. Within a few weeks, in January 1886, Terry married Hill.

Sharon's heirs sued to have the original marriage document thrown out by the federal court, to ensure that Hill would never get her hands on Sharon's estate. Hill harangued Justice Field, again out for his summer appellate court supervision. When Field ordered that she be removed from the courtroom, Hill struck a federal marshal on the face. Terry told the marshal, "No man shall touch my wife," and when told to stand back, slugged the marshal. As Hill scratched anyone in sight and Terry swore and pulled out his Bowie knife, they were removed from the courtroom. Field declared them guilty of contempt of court, and they both spent time in prison.

Mr. and Mrs. Terry hated the judges and particularly despised Justice Field. Both were quoted at length in the newspapers. Terry talked about seeing judges in their graves and killing Fields. Hill's rants also included killing Field and Circuit Judge Lorenzo Sawyer. Field didn't care, but in Washington, officials were alarmed. The US attorney general ensured that a US Marshal, David Neagle, was assigned to protect Field when he arrived in California for the summer court session in 1889.

On August 13, Neagle accompanied Field on the train ride from Los Angeles to San Francisco. Neagle spotted the Terrys boarding the train at night at a Fresno stop, alerted Justice Field, and wired ahead to the morning train stop in Lathrop that there might be trouble. In the morning, Neagle tried to persuade Field to stay on board for breakfast, but when the justice insisted on dining in the station, Neagle went with him.

The Terrys entered the station dining room. Mrs. Terry spotted Field and ran out to the train to get her satchel (where a pistol had been found several times over the years during past searches). David Terry was seated, then got up, went around Field, and slapped the justice on both sides of the face. Neagle shouted, "Stop! Stop! I am an officer," but Terry appeared to reach for his well-known Bowie knife. Neagle fired twice. Terry died instantly. Mrs. Terry ran in, an open satchel with a loaded revolver in hand. She began screaming.

Field, who hadn't moved during the incident, was briefly arrested under a warrant sworn by Mrs. Terry. His release was ordered by California's governor who didn't want the disgrace of the trial of a Supreme Court justice.

Neagle was to be tried for murder in California, but Federal Circuit Court Judge Sawyer ordered his release. The case was appealed to the US Supreme Court, where Justice Field recused himself. In the decision *In re Neagle,* 135 U.S. 1 (1890), the court held that since the Constitution charged the executive branch of government with faithful execution of the law, the appointment of bodyguards for Supreme Court justices fulfilled the law, and that marshals had powers equal to and the same protections as sheriffs.

Neagle was free, and his shooting of Terry to protect the federal officer in his charge became a precedent for protecting those acting in the line of duty. Justice Field sat on the US Supreme Court for thirty-four years, the longest serving justice in history. Sarah Althea Hill Terry, violently insane, was committed to Stockton State Hospital where she died forty-five years later. Never far away from her, David Terry was buried in the Stockton Rural Cemetery.

SOURCES

In *The Magnificent Rogues of San Francisco* (Palo Alto, Calif.: Pacific Books, Publishers, 1998), Charles F. Adams includes a chapter about the "strange and singular life" of "David Terry: The Judge Who Became a Public Enemy."

The Rivals: William Gwin, David Broderick, and the Birth of California (New York: Crown Publishers, Inc., 1994), by the late University of California, Berkeley rhetoric professor, Arthur Quinn, is a fine, meaty, and evocative read about California politics as the new state found its bearings politically, and how it and the major personalities dealt with the slavery issue. *California: A History of the Golden State* (Garden City, New York: Doubleday & Company, Inc., 1972), by Warren A. Beck and David A. Williams, reveals the ins and outs of California law on dueling, what actually happened in "affairs of honor," and why the Broderick-Terry duel had such a significant effect on pro-slavery sympathies in the state. Orator Edward D. Baker's complete eulogy for Broderick is found in Joseph Wallace's *Sketch of the Life and Public Services of Edward D. Baker* (Springfield, Ill.: Journal Company, 1870).

Brooks W. MacCracken's article, "Althea and the Judges," in *American Heritage Magazine* (June, 1967, Vol. 18, Issue 4), uses his talent as a storyteller to describe Sarah Althea Hill-Terry's life and legal cases in detail. The US Marshals Service is proud of the precedent, upheld in the US Supreme Court, of justified use of force in the line of duty while protecting a federal official. The Neagle case is described and illustrated with historic documents and portraits at its website, www.justice.gov/marshals/history/neagle.

CHAPTER 5

Modoc War

Captain Jack versus the United States

Not every bad guy sets out to be a jerk. Some people enter the state of jerk-ness reluctantly, lashing out when cornered or fenced in. Desperation and futility also play a part.

One such man was Kientpoos, a leader among an isolated, self-sustaining people in far northern California. When his followers were forcibly uprooted by nineteenth-century United States government Indian policy and made to live with their enemies, this chief led some of his tribe back to their homeland. Chased by the army during the only major Indian war in California, the small band of Native Americans hid and resisted capture for many months. Despite the Indians' pleas, a group of American government jerks had decided that there would be no agreement to let them stay where their ancestors had lived.

Kientpoos (Kintpuash)—known to the whites as Captain Jack—goaded to commit murder by younger Modoc men, had little left to lose and so struck out violently at the unarmed military negotiators who would have held him to the government's involuntary displacement policy. Was he to be tried as an enemy combatant by the military or for murder in a civilian court? His fate would be the same: Captain Jack paid the ultimate price on the gallows for his jerk deed.

It was 10:00 a.m. on October 3, 1873, and Kientpoos did not have much longer to wait. He could see ropes ending in nooses at the end of a beam suspended from the Fort Klamath stockade. One was for him.

Perhaps Elder Wife, Younger Wife Lizzie, and Daughter Rosie, only three years old now, would live on? Kientpoos, who his military captors knew as Captain Jack, would never know. At 10:28 a.m., with a crowd of deathly silent Modoc tribespeople watching, Jack and three other Modoc warriors were "hanged by the neck until they be dead." Then the screaming began. But Captain Jack and three other Modocs, Schonchin John, Boston Charley, and Black Jim, were beyond hearing anything.

Shortly after, a *San Francisco Chronicle* reporter who was present at Fort Klamath in southern Oregon for the hanging noticed something amiss in a tent: Some sort of surgery had taken place. The heads of the four executed Modocs had been cut off. They were, the reporter was assured, not severed in a barbarian desecration, but were destined for the Army Military Museum in Washington, DC

For Captain Jack, it was the final indignity, the true end of the Modoc War, the only major Indian war fought in California. His had been the brilliant strategy of hiding a small number of his people in the lava beds' inhospitable terrain while inflicting significant damage and casualties on the US Army that pursued them. The lava beds in extreme northern California were part of the traditional homeland of his people, the Modocs.

The "war" had begun in winter, less than a year before, on November 29, 1872. Indian country superintendents and Indian agents in southern Oregon and the army concluded that the Modocs would be most vulnerable during the bone-chilling cold and strong winds and occasional snows that swept their lands in winter. It was a bad miscalculation. The Modocs had lived with the extreme winter weather and climate for centuries in a landscape they knew well. They had also been working on settlers' ranches, allowing some of their daughters to marry whites, and adopted American clothing for almost twenty years. They knew their enemy.

The Modocs had encountered the trailblazers first: Captain John Frémont had passed through their lands in early 1846 and retaliated against Modocs for killings committed by Modoc rivals, the Klamaths. When the first whites arrived during the Oregon Trail migration in the late 1840s, some emigrants had chosen to go by a route along the north side of ninety-five-thousand-acre Tule Lake that along with Clear Lake and Lower Klamath Lake (in Oregon) was the heart of the Modoc people's homeland. The Lost River, with its wetlands and watershed, flowed in a north-south arc from Clear Lake to Tule Lake. The lake and river waters drew thousands of ducks, other waterfowl, and spawning fish. The Modocs gathered roots, *wocas* (water lily) seeds, berries, nuts, and bird eggs, and the men hunted deer, bighorn sheep, and pronghorn antelope. They made boats of wood or tule reeds.

Spring meant construction of temporary rounded-ceiling huts made of tule reeds not far from the Lost River. As summer progressed, they moved higher into forests south of the lava beds for hunting and food gathering. As the season turned, with food preservation complete, the Modocs prepared to move their food and families to their winter shelters, earthen lodges on lake or river banks.

Their traditional life rhythms that included storytelling to pass on traditions and women's intricately woven baskets from tule reeds and sagebrush bark began to shatter with the coming of the first white immigrants. Gold discoveries to the west brought even more settlers and prospectors and their vulnerable wagon trains. In 1852, Modoc attacks led to several revenge attacks by white settlers led by Ben Wright, from Yreka, the major population center south of Oregon, to roust out and kill Modocs. Young Kientpoos would have heard of these battles and ambushes and may have witnessed killings that sometimes included taking of scalps by both sides. Wright's posse destroyed at least one whole Modoc village. Several of the survivors would remember that massacre when Captain Jack made their stand against white authority twenty years later.

Some of the settlers surging into southern Oregon and the Modoc areas just across the border in California took traditional lands and free access away from the Modocs. The land was fenced. Herds of cattle grazed a landscape where large groups of animals had never been. Property rights that whites enforced had no meaning in the traditional tribal system of sharing and cooperating within the group. Some settlers complained that Modocs would appear, enter their houses or cabins, and expect food to be handed to them, a situation the whites deemed harassment of their women and a threat.

Although the Modocs shared some traditions with other tribes, the Klamaths (in Oregon), the Shastas (at the foot of Mount Shasta in northern California), and the Rogue Rivers (in Oregon), whites tended to see all Indians as the same. Yet, Modoc lands and customs made them a distinct people.

The pressure of white settlement by miners, homesteaders, and those filing claims to lands considered open to new arrivals was strong and the US government began to assist them. A lawyer and Indian agent in Yreka in 1863 who the Modoc trusted told them they would be able to stay on their lands on the Lost River, even though he knew the government was making other arrangements. On October 14, 1864, US commissioners and Klamath and Modoc tribal chiefs concluded a treaty where the Indians ceded "all their right, title, interest and claim in and to all lands" outside the Klamath Reservation that had been set aside in southern Oregon, agreed to settle there and never leave, be obedient, and maintain peaceable relations with whites. Among the Modoc chiefs, Captain Jack hesitated but finally agreed. The US Senate ratified the treaty in 1866, and the Modocs, including Jack, agreed to the amended treaty terms on December 10, 1869.

No one had listened to protestations that the Modocs and Klamaths, though in close proximity in their home ranges, were traditional enemies. Yet, Kientpoos went north with the Modocs to the Klamath Reservation, located at Upper Klamath Lake. There, the Modocs were, by their own description that was confirmed by Indian agents charged with their care, "harassed" by the rival Klamaths whose reservation was actually their traditional tribal land. Food and supplies promised as part of the resettlement treaty terms were not provided. They were cut off from their seasonal migrations, fishing, hunting, and traditional lands they knew. Most Modocs stayed at the urging of the main chief, Schonchin. Kientpoos left the Klamath Reservation to return to the Lost River with a group of followers several times and was always persuaded to return.

Tired of being harassed by the Klamaths even when the Modocs had been moved to another location on the reservation and when the money to buy their food was terminated, Kientpoos and his band of 371 dissenters left again in February 1870, determined to go to Lost River and reestablish themselves. This time, they would not settle for less than their own land. But that land was now settled by whites.

Meanwhile, on March 3, 1871, in Washington, DC, President Ulysses S. Grant signed the Indian Appropriation Act, his Indian peace policy, that nullified existing Indian treaties and made Indians direct wards of the United States. In mid-1871, Oregon Superintendent for Indian Affairs Alfred B. Meacham told Captain Jack to remain where he was on the Lost River until something might be worked out to create a Modoc reservation there. Friendly lawyers in Yreka also advised Captain Jack to remain peacefully at his Lost River location.

But time was running out and pressure was building. Meacham had changed his mind by January 1872, and before he left office, he sent Army Brigadier General E. R. S. Canby, commander of the Division of the Pacific, a request for a military force to remove Jack's group and take them back to the reservation. His letter enclosed a petition signed by forty-five purported Lost River settlers. When Canby denied the request, Meacham wrote back, "They have not kept their part of the agreement and hence have forfeited any claim they might have had to forbearance."

What worried the Office of Indian Affairs and its agents was settlers' legal "pre-emption" of the Modocs lands and white complaints about thefts and threats. They worried that a precedent would be set for other tribes if Captain Jack and his people were allowed to stay where they were. Their worst fear was sparking a confederation of defiant Native Americans conducting mass warfare against the United States.

During the spring and summer and into September, Jack was visited by military officers. The new superintendent for Indian Affairs at Salem, Oregon, Thomas Benton Odeneal, agreed with Meacham that the only decision could be removal back to the Klamath Reservation to a designated area, the Yainax Station, at some distance from most contact with the Klamaths, and that the leaders should be sent elsewhere until they cooperated with the government's program. The Indian agents met with the chiefs. Captain Jack, still at Lost Creek, made a speech:

> *We are good people, and will not kill or frighten anybody. We want peace and friendship ... I do not want to live upon the reservation, for the Indians there are poorly clothed, suffer from hunger, and even have to leave the reservation sometimes to make a living. We are willing to have whites live in our country, but do not want them to locate on the west side and near the mouth of the Lost River, where we have our winter camps. The settlers are continually lying about my people and trying to make trouble.*

In June, Superintendent Odeneal reported the contacts to Commissioner of Indian Affairs F. A. Walker, describing the Modoc leaders as "desperadoes—brave, daring and reckless." On July 6, 1872, Commissioner Walker approved the Modocs' transportation back to the Klamath Reservation, "peaceably if you can, but forcibly if you must." They waited until winter.

On November 28, under orders, Major John Green ordered Captain James Jackson to lead a small contingent south from Fort Klamath to the Lost River Modoc villages, one on each side of the river, for a show of force. At the first village, Modoc leaders were ordered to surrender and come forward, but the men emerged with guns and the soldiers fired. A battle ensued, and the Modocs were driven away. The war had begun.

The other village was attacked, too, and armed settlers helped the soldiers. The Modocs fled. Captain Jack's group and the women and children in boats went across the river at night while Hooker Jim's five warriors rode around the lake, killing fourteen white settlers on the way.

While reluctant to have with him men who the whites would come after as murderers, Kientpoos led the Modocs into the lava beds, soon joined by another group from Hot Creek. Kientpoos set up the winter camp in the lava beds in a natural formation that acted as a fortification and living quarters, later dubbed Captain Jack's Stronghold.

The army was in an unfamiliar territory and landscape. The Stronghold, close to the banks of Tule Lake's water supply and food resources, was a natural fortification formed by ancient lava flows, and magma movement had created lava tubes. Some were filled with magma and pushed up and out against a crust, forming actual rugged domes used as Modoc sentry points. Others sagged or collapsed into vertical-walled pits where large boulders tumbled in, offering cave-like shelters to Jack's band. Surrounding most of the Stronghold were large lava-made fissures, treacherous for anyone attempting to cross. There was a small, flat, natural corral space, which the Modocs used to confine beef cattle they had captured as they moved toward the Stronghold. And, unbeknownst to the army, there was an almost straight, relatively unfissured route south out of the Stronghold, should the need arise.

A combined force of about four hundred men, including army soldiers, California and Oregon one-month volunteers, settlers, and townspeople, assembled to attack the Stronghold. It was a bitterly cold and extremely foggy winter morning on January 17, 1873, when the first troops moved out to set up a line of skirmish. Modocs waited and began sniper fire to draw the troops toward the worst fissured area. From higher vantage points the Modocs fired into the fog at the soldiers' assumed positions. It went on until 10:00 p.m. that night, with several groups of soldiers wandering, taking fire, and unable to pinpoint the Modocs' defensive points. The army counted thirty-seven dead; no Modocs had died.

The resident Modoc shaman, Curley Headed Doctor, had predicted that the Modocs would be invincible. After their victory, they believed him.

Army leadership brought Brigadier General Canby and Colonel Alvan Gillem to personally handle the campaign, and for three months, Canby followed his plan to gradually compress the Modocs into the Stronghold with no possible escape. More troops were moved into camps near the Stronghold. At the same time, a peace commission had been having occasional meetings with the Modocs to discuss the tribe's two demands: a reservation of their own on their traditional homeland and a reprieve for those Modocs involved in the earlier settler murders. The Modocs noticed the growing number of troops setting up camps closer and closer to the Stronghold. And, all the time, reporters were photographing from army positions, documenting the Stronghold geography with images or accurate sketches to tell their readers their tale of Indians resisting in a raw-as-hell landscape.

The Modocs, especially the younger men, were getting cocky, restless, and disgusted with the peace commission and General Canby. The commission did not seem to be doing anything while the military simultaneously closed in. In early April, one of the young men, supported by others, told Kientpoos that he should kill General Canby at the next meeting, a show of force that they thought would take care of both the peace commission and military problem at the same time and get them respect. After all, the shaman had said they were invincible.

Kientpoos strongly refused, but the others goaded him by calling him a coward, physically shoving him to the ground, and made him wear women's clothes. In the end, a humiliated Kientpoos agreed to kill Canby himself and called for a formal peace commission meeting on April 11.

As the meeting was set up, one of Jack's followers told his cousin, Tobey (Winema) Riddle, the Modoc woman and translator

Modocs scalping and torturing prisoners
FROM LIBRARY OF CONGRESS PRINTS AND PHOTOGRAPHS DIVISION. ILLUSTRATION FROM *HARPER'S WEEKLY*, MAY 17, 1873.

who was married to white settler Frank Riddle, about the murder plot. Tobey Riddle pleaded with Canby and the others not to go, but he reportedly said that the Modocs would not dare molest them because they felt the whites controlled the situation. General Canby, peace commission head Alfred Meacham, Methodist minister Eleazar Thomas from Petaluma, Indian Sub-Agent Leroy Dyar, the Riddles as interpreters, and two Modocs who had been visiting the Riddles to keep up appearances that communications were ongoing, set out for the peace tent where scouts had reported five unarmed Modocs waiting. When they arrived, the Modocs were armed.

Canby told the Modocs that he was there for their protection and, for a while, the men sat and smoked cigars Canby had brought with him. Formal discussions began with the Riddles translating. Jack said the Modocs were tired of war and wanted the troops withdrawn. Canby countered that the soldiers were there to protect them and couldn't be withdrawn unless President Grant ordered it.

Suddenly, shots were heard in the distance, and two young armed Modoc men, Barncho and Slolux, came up behind Canby's group. When Canby asked what this was about, Jack turned his back and said he didn't want to talk. Schonchin John yelled that they wanted a reserve on Hot Creek. Captain Jack turned around, raised his pistol, said in Modoc, "All ready," and misfired. His second shot hit Canby point-blank in the face. The general staggered off and fell on the rough rocks, where Jack and another man finished killing him. Boston Charley shot Reverend Thomas. Schonchin John fired at Meacham who fell, apparently dead. Bald, Meacham was saved from Boston Charley's attempt to completely scalp him by Tobey Riddle who protected Meacham with her body. Dyar was pursued, then fired a derringer, and got away. Frank Riddle rode for help and later Tobey appeared at the army camp.

Captain Jack and the other Modoc perpetrators fled back into the Stronghold. The Modocs expected immediate army retaliation, but the troops were disorganized. It took four days to begin a second Stronghold siege to cut the Modocs off from water. When the army finally entered the Stronghold on April 17, it was empty. Captain Jack had led the Modocs south over the narrow escape route through the lava beds.

The news reporters on the scene filed their stories, vying by means of bribing riders to take their tales to Yreka. Far away from the battleground, there had been some sympathy for Captain Jack's "heroic" Modocs who wanted their own land and fought from their own fortress, less than seventy men against a much more numerous military force. The headlines soon screamed about Modoc treachery.

There was fighting as the Modocs fled further south. Then, a Modoc surprise attack failed, and the Indians fled without their horses and provisions. With their invincibility shattered, the Modocs began to argue. The group split up, and Hooker Jim led his own group back toward Hot Creek. Surprised by soldiers along the way, Hooker Jim, still wanted for the original settlers' murder when the war started, surrendered and then organized a Modoc party to track down Captain Jack for the army.

They found him and a few others at Willow Creek. It was June 1, 1873.

Captain Jack surrendered his gun and with it his life. The Modoc War was over.

The 155 captured Modocs—forty-four men, forty-nine women, and sixty-two children—were put in a purpose-built stockade at Fort Klamath. A shackled Captain Jack's only comment to an army colonel was that his legs had given out. The colonel had a scaffold ready for summary execution within a few days, but by June 9, the US attorney general had decided that the Modocs had made war and could be tried and punished by a military court convened as a military commission.

Six Modocs who had been involved in the peace commission murders, including Captain Jack, faced the military commission panel with no representative of their own, from July 1 to 9. All six were found guilty of the murders of General Canby and Reverend Thomas and of assault on Meacham and Dyar with intent to kill in violation of the laws of war. Despite cries for more blood or for mercy by those who thought that bad white men had instigated the war, President Grant approved the military commission's sentence: "To be hanged by the neck until they be dead." Grant also granted life imprisonment in Alcatraz Military Prison for Barncho and Slolux, with orders that they were not to be told until they were not put on the gallows platform. Their graves were dug with the others'.

The night before Captain Jack died, he and Schonchin John, Black Jim, Boston Charley, Barncho, and Slolux sat silent on the stockade floor as their families chanted the last song. The next morning, the noose abruptly took the life of Kientpoos, Modoc leader, the man who murdered an unarmed man.

POSTSCRIPT

In return for his assistance in the capture of Captain Jack, Hooker Jim and the other Modocs who had murdered the settlers at the beginning of the war were not tried for the murders.

Only a few Modocs stayed on the Klamath Reservation. Within two weeks, most of the survivors, including Kientpoos's daughter, Rosie, had been taken by wagon to Yreka, where they were put on a train and shipped off to Fort McPherson, Nebraska. The Modoc hunter-gatherers were sent further south to Indian Territory (Oklahoma) near the Quapaw Agency and given a small tract of land to farm. The Indian agents were Quakers, and not all were honest. In the end, many Modocs became Quakers. In later years, a few returned to the Klamath Agency. Most of Captain Jack's Modoc band, including his daughter, remained in Oklahoma. Rosie Jack died the spring after her father was hanged.

SOURCES

Few "jerks" are memorialized by the government they fought, but Captain Jack's Stronghold and its natural caves are preserved in Lava Beds National Monument and interpreted by the US National

Captain Jack's cave in the lava beds during the Modoc War
FROM LIBRARY OF CONGRESS PRINTS AND PHOTOGRAPHS DIVISION. ILLUSTRATION FROM *HARPER'S WEEKLY*, JUNE 28, 1873.

Park Service in conjunction with Modoc tribal groups. The Lava Beds National Monument website includes a lot of information about the Modoc Homeland (www.nps.gov/labe/historyculture/modochomeland.htm) and the war that involved Captain Jack, including the text of *Modoc War: Its Military History & Topography,* by Erwin N. Thompson (Sacramento, Calif.: Argus Books, 1971); online at www.nps.gov/history/history/online_books/labe.

The US government's own blunt internal discussion of the looming dispute with Captain Jack's holdout group was documented at the time by Thomas Benton Odeneal, the superintendent of Indian Affairs at Salem, Oregon, in *The Modoc War; Statement of Its Origins and Causes Containing an Account of the Treaty, Copies of Petitions, and Official Correspondence* (Portland, Or.: "Bulletin" Steam Book and Job Printing Office, 1873, in the Southern Oregon Hannon Library Digital Collection, Tribal materials, http://soda.sou .edu/Data/Library1/020925c1.pdf). Letters between the commissioner of the Department of the Interior's Office of Indian Affairs, superintendents of Indian affairs in Oregon, local Indian agency translators, and officers of the US Army were compiled, Odeneal says, after local settlers requested that a document be prepared to counter false impressions of the press and people on the American East Coast.

Jeff Riddle, who as a ten-year-old boy accompanied his Modoc mother, (Winema) Tobey Riddle, and white father, Frank, in the peace commission negotiations, later wrote a memoir that evokes all his horror at the inevitable end he knew would come: *The Indian History of the Modoc War and the Causes That Led to It* (San Francisco: Marnell Co., 1914, with many recent facsimile imprints). PBS's *History Detectives* Season 8, Episode 9, Segment 3 (http://video.pbs.org/video/1565249292) is about Modoc War heroine, Tobey Riddle, brought to life by a search for a Modoc basket maker. Diablo Valley College, Pleasant Hill, California, history professor Rebecca Bales covered "Winema and the Modoc War: One Woman's Struggle for Peace" in the National Archives and Records Administration magazine (*Prologue,* Vol. 37, No. 1, Spring 2005).

Richard Dillon's *Burnt-Out Fires* (Englewood Cliffs, New Jersey: Prentice-Hall, Inc., 1973) adds historical perspective to the raw details of the story, with a deft touch for the storytelling. Professor Arthur Quinn's last book, *Hell with the Fire Out: A History of the Modoc War* (Boston: Faber and Faber, Inc., 1997), weaves history with the stark emotions felt by participants. The US Geographical Survey Circular 838 includes an analysis of Modoc defensive strategy in "Captain Jack's Stronghold—The Geological Events that created a Natural Fortress" (Aaron C. Waters, www.cr.nps .gov/history/online_books/geology/publications/circ/838/sec6.htm).

CHAPTER 6

Sympathy for a Bandido
Californio *Tiburcio Vásquez:*
Villain, Lover, Legend

Some jerks are the sort of bad guys who create legends. Bandits like the fictional Robin Hood exude noble motives, emanate style, and have enemies who justify a robber's career and make him a hero. The reality of a bandit's life, including that of a notorious bandit like *californio* Tiburcio Vásquez, was steeped in blood, hard living, and constant fear of betrayal. Vásquez wasn't quite forty years old when his deeds caught up with him for the final time. The irony is that this bad guy, with a well-documented career of crime and time in prison, was a patriotic hero to many Mexican Americans in California.

Vásquez's early life coincided with the end of the calm period of cattle ranchos and sturdy adobes, frequent fiestas, dancing señoritas, and a closely integrated society during the brief time that Mexico ruled Alta California from 1821 to 1846. By the end of Vásquez's life in 1875, the *californio* culture he came from had been subsumed by an overwhelming number of English-speaking Americans. Those Anglos's striving and roughshod brashness may have pushed a fun-loving, good-looking young man with an eye for the girls and a readiness to fight to a lifetime of crime.

Outlaw Tiburcio Vásquez always swore that he had never, ever, murdered anyone himself. He may have been the only one who believed it.

Endless robberies, horse stealing, and alleged murders finally triggered California Governor Newton Booth's offer of a reward for the capture or the corpse of the infamous bandido,

Tiburcio Vásquez. Too often the elusive repeat offender had gone to ground with his gang. The desperado was persuasive with his gun, threatening those who didn't help him willingly like most of his large family and his numerous friends did. Vásquez gang members were extremely loyal to their chief, and he to them. It was going to take the reward, California's best manhunter, a traitor, and luck to bring the outlaw Vásquez to the justice he so richly deserved.

Governor Booth guaranteed $2,000 for the body or $3,000 for the live bandit. Booth later increased the reward to a princely $8,000 for Vásquez's capture. Even friends might think twice about not turning him in for that kind of money.

His extended family had always protected Vásquez even though no one endorsed his actions. Vásquez was always giving the men valuable watches—stolen goods—as a token of his appreciation. Then, he went too far. A ladies' man, Vásquez got his own niece Felicita pregnant, infuriating his blood relatives and the legion of relations by marriage. And, there were other women who felt betrayed by Vásquez, too, women he had bedded who were jealous.

Vasquez's effrontery pushed too far and his life started to unravel. He was holed up with Georgios Caralambos, known as Greek George, on May 14, 1874, at George's country adobe, not far from La Brea's tar pits in Los Angeles County. George's wife, Cornelia López, was Vásquez's cousin, but she was also related to the young man who had truly loved the ravished niece, Felicita. Even more: Cornelia's sister was another of Vásquez's lovers. It had gotten too complicated.

No one ever admitted to telling the governor's designated manhunter who had been appointed to head the posse, Alameda County Sheriff Henry N. "Harry" Morse, where Vásquez could be found, but Morse's informant was correct this time. Morse, Spanish-speaking and a dead-accurate shot, had pursued Vásquez more than 2,700 miles around California by his own estimate. And he would have nabbed the bandit, except for the professional courtesy he extended to the Los Angeles County sheriff in whose jurisdiction Vásquez had gone to ground. If only his colleague, Sheriff William Rowland, had believed his tip from the anonymous source. . . .

But Rowland hadn't shrugged off the information, just Morse the messenger who had already left and gone back to northern California. Whoever physically captured Vásquez would get the reward. It was time to cultivate sources, to find someone who would "peach" and squeal on Vásquez, someone angry enough at the bandido and who wanted a share of the reward's easy money. Rowland needed a cooperative traitor. And it probably would be someone outside the close-knit and protective *californios* or Mexicans. They regarded Vásquez as a folk hero for robbing and attacking oppressor Anglos, even though Hispanics had also been hold-up victims.

Vásquez's fights were with men, not women. He was known among friends, especially those of the fairer sex, as a guitar-playing poet and balladeer, charming, and usually chivalrous. He had adored his mother and was close to his sisters.

Dark-haired, light-skinned Vásquez didn't start out bad. Not every boy starts out to be a robber and a murderer. Vásquez always said that his mother, Doña Guadalupe, had given him her blessing when he was seventeen. That's when he told her he was going to do something different with his life. She was a devout Catholic who attended Mass every day, so he just may not have elaborated on his chosen path, that of bandido. But he was simply not one to settle down to a life as a *vaquero* (cowboy), shepherd, farmer, or shop owner.

The Vásquez family had lived in Monterey along California's central coast during the Spanish and Mexican eras. Vásquez was born in that provincial capital, a citizen of far-off Mexico, on April, 10, 1835. Vasquez's distant ancestors were from Spain, Africa, and Native America. His great grandparents and grandparents had made the Spanish settlers' trek from Mexico to California with Conquistador Juan Bautista de Anza in 1775–1776. Vásquez and his typically large family of numerous siblings, aunts, uncles, cousins, and relatives by marriage thought of themselves as *californios,* people of California, rather than as Mexicans. Everyone knew each other, even if the richer rancho owners who claimed the purest Spanish bloodlines didn't socialize or intermarry with the rest. Vásquez's middle-class family was respectable, and through the generations, the men had served as soldiers and administrators, or as rancher-farmers like his father, Hermenegildo.

A town had grown around the provincial capital, Monterey, with adobe buildings for homes and places of business. Although his father had a small rancho on the Pajaro River near San Juan Bautista, and like other *californio* young men, Tiburcio was an experienced *vaquero*, a working cowboy, the life of a cattle rancher or shepherd held no interest.

Instead, he loved horse races and gambling. He also enjoyed the fandangos, dance halls where young women sang, played the guitar, and entertained the men. When he was seventeen, he ran a fandango in a small Monterey adobe where there was gambling with cards and plenty of alcohol. His one-time fiancée may have been one of the dance hall girls.

Montereños' lives were changing dramatically. They became American citizens in 1846 with the signing of the Treaty of Guadalupe Hidalgo. The 1848–1849 Gold Rush brought white men, Anglos, disembarking from ships in Monterey's harbor. Most sailors or prospectors were rough men just passing through, with no respect for the darker-skinned residents or their women. Soon, the *californios* were only 5 percent of California's population, suffering economically as the newcomers impinged on their rancho way of life and denigrated their traditional culture.

Vásquez later claimed that his choice to be a bandit stemmed from the constant mauling of local women in his fandango by Anglos. On September 2, 1854, Vásquez and some friends got into a fight at someone's fandango. Details were unclear, but someone shot the popular local constable William Hardmount in the head. Whether guilty of the murder or not, Vásquez left town and took up the life of a bandido, a robber with no permanent residence, indulging in gambling and seducing women.

He was not the only bandido with a reputation: The most famous, Joaquín Murrieta, had arrived with the Gold Rush influx of men from Sonora, Mexico. With others, including fellow Sonoran Claudio Feliz, Murrieta robbed and killed from the Mother Lode through the San Joaquin Valley and on down to Los Angeles. Juan Soto, whose gang Vásquez occasionally joined, had solidified Sheriff Morse's reputation as a fearless bandit hunter. Morse finally shot the remorseless murderer Soto dead in a guns-blazing shootout in 1871. Wherever he was, a gang leader like Vásquez recruited eager young men for one or two forays. When the young *californios* or Mexican-Americans returned to their ranching, sheep herding, or farming, no one would be the wiser and the young men might be a little richer.

In the beginning, Vásquez hired on to short-term legitimate jobs as a *vaquero* or shepherd, even driving cattle from Ventura to markets in Monterey, but he didn't hold regular jobs for long. He was riding with outlaw gangs, stealing horses or cattle, or holing up in secluded canyons to evade capture. Other times, he imposed on the hospitality of relatives and friends who liked him or others who hated Anglos and the plethora of corrupt lawmen, judges, and lawyers who seemed to have come with them.

In Los Angeles County in July 1857, Vásquez and two Indians were arrested for stealing horses. For a first conviction, he received an especially stiff sentence of five years for grand larceny because of the notorious deeds of other horse-rustling bandidos. When he arrived in three-year-old San Quentin State Prison on August 26, 1857, five feet and three-eighths inches tall, Prisoner 1217 was listed as Tiburcio Basquez.

Conditions were harsh and overcrowded, with bad food. Basquez/Vásquez escaped from San Quentin four times. In June 1859, when he and another convict friend were caught stealing two horses in Amador County and sent back to San Quentin, Vásquez had another year added to his prison term. In September, the bandido and twenty other Anglo convicts loading bricks onto a prison sloop tried to seize the ship. After each escape, Vásquez was tied onto a support and lashed on the back with up to one hundred fifty strokes. On January 16, 1861, Vásquez and twenty other convicts took the deputy warden and others hostage and fought their way through San Quentin's main gate. Escapees were quickly hunted down and fired upon at the deputy warden's order. Vásquez and most of the survivors were badly wounded and were returned to prison. In the fourth escape in July 1862, California's lieutenant governor who was an ex-officio warden was taken as a hostage. Dozens of escaped convicts were recaptured, among them Vásquez, a prison break planner and ringleader. Vásquez finished his six years of imprisonment in August 1863.

Most of his family had moved inland to San Juan Bautista, and for a while, Vásquez worked as a *vaquero* on a nearby rancho during the day and frequented the gambling houses and fandangos at night. Eventually he moved into a life of gambling and horse racing at large local quicksilver mines, and then began robbing individuals in their homes and on the road as a highwayman. As a gang member, he stole horses, helped rebrand them, and moved them far away for resale. His profits were spent on fine, elegant clothes and fancy high-heeled boots for visits to places of entertainment, fandangos, bordellos, or gambling establishments. A fluent English and Spanish speaker, he sometimes translated for witnesses of crimes that he may have committed, ensuring that the testimony wouldn't implicate him. Everywhere Vásquez went, he seduced local girls.

By 1865, Tiburcio Vásquez was in Marin and Sonoma Counties, riding as far north as sparsely populated Mendocino County for some rustling. For a while he was based in Petaluma as a sometime shepherd, an apparent excuse to help other San Quentin alumni rob a Main Street general store by cutting in from underneath. Elsewhere, the gang broke into safes and took the contents. Vásquez and his fellow bandits were after guns, ammunition, swords, knives, watches, jewelry, coins, fine clothes, saddles, and any horses or cattle they could steal.

Petaluma Marshal James Knowles had been arresting Vásquez's confederates one by one, and perhaps they "peached," because on December 17, 1866, he locked Vásquez in the Sonoma County Jail. By January 18, 1867, Vásquez had been convicted for burgling the Petaluma general store and pleaded guilty to grand larceny for stealing a rifle.

He was sent back to San Quentin for two consecutive two-year terms. In San Quentin, Vásquez met old robber band friends and newer *californio* and Mexican convicts. There was cultural under-standing, criminal knowledge, and Vásquez had become known as a desperado who said he acted for them, the ignored and dis-placed minority, inside and out of prison. The recent Goodwin Act mandated time off a sentence for good behavior, so there were no escape attempts, and Vasquez walked free on June 4, 1870. He was thirty-five-years old.

He returned briefly to San Juan Bautista, though Doña Gua-dalupe had died the year before. There were a lot of changes in that part of central California, a flood of people arriving by rail-road and new cities such as Salinas and Hollister had appeared with the influx. The *californio* culture was being overwhelmed. Yet the rough countryside, with canyons and places to hide, lured the *californio* and Mexican ex-convicts who formed loose gangs under various leaders, including Juan Soto and Vásquez. To the usual horse thefts and robberies, Vásquez's gang added masked stage-coach hold-ups, where the Wells Fargo express box with gold coins was the target. The highwaymen became more and more brazen, sometimes not even bothering to wear masks.

In late August 1873, Vásquez decided to rob a stagecoach and then rob a store nearby in tiny Tres Pinos (now Paicines), south of Hollister in San Benito County. One of his gang, Albon Leiva, had figured he'd be fingered for a recent murder and sold his adobe, preparing to move to Mexico. He needed more cash. Leiva paid another gang member to drive his wife, Rosario, and the children south in a wagon while Leiva joined Vásquez to "earn" a share of the bandidos' take by joining in the robbery.

The Tres Pinos store acted as a supply center, stagecoach stop, and US mail delivery point for letters and newspapers. There was also a hotel, blacksmith, livery stable, and saddlery in the hamlet. When the stagecoach appeared on the Hollister-San Benito route after the Tres Pinos stop, Vásquez recognized an assistant superintendent of one of the mines who he liked and he decided not to rob the stage or its occupants. When Vásquez and his companions regrouped in Tres Pinos with the two advance men who included Albon Leiva, all hell broke loose.

Store occupants, the clerk, the hotel keeper and his wife, and others were ordered onto the floor, pistol-whipped, and tied up. Outside, a local Portuguese shepherd didn't understand the English "halt!" and was shot to death. A blacksmith's son trying to run was beaten with a shotgun. A deaf teamster arriving at the store heard nothing but saw the guns, ran into the livery barn, and was shot in the back, killed by Vásquez. Leiva told the hotelman and his wife to stay inside the hotel and they wouldn't be shot. As they started closing the door, with others coming through, Vásquez fired through the door into the hotel keeper's chest, killing the man, who fell into his screaming wife's arms.

The bandits got the valuables, and then sat down to beer and a meal. Several hours after they had arrived, Vásquez's gang stole some horses, took their loot and some new clothes, and rode away.

Local people were outraged at the murders of innocent people and there was a national outcry. The governor announced a reward for the capture of gang members. The newspapers labeled it the worst bandit gang since Joaquín Murrieta. Santa Clara County Sheriff John Adams, working outside of his area, was finally able to persuade some men to join a posse.

Vásquez, Leiva, and another henchman, along with Rosario Leiva who had joined them, fled south. They ended up in a remote canyon east of Elizabeth Lake at the base of the San Gabriel Mountains. Leiva, suspicious of Vásquez and Rosario, agreed to go back to Elizabeth Lake for provisions, but instead returned to find the bandido in bed with Rosario. Leiva denounced Vásquez, stayed the night, and then left with Rosario the next morning. Rosario, along with the children and some of the Tres Pinos loot, was left to fend for herself while Leiva rode to Los Angeles to turn himself in, without telling her.

Sheriff Adams and his tiny posse, riding almost nonstop, got word of Vásquez's location in the secluded canyon. Adams wired Los Angeles Sheriff Rowland who, with the information Leiva had given to his deputy, was already en route to rendezvous with Adams. They followed tracks up the canyon and found stolen horses and finally Vásquez with his fellow bandido. A gun battle ensued, but even at so close a range, the outlaws were able to flee. Adams and his group followed Rosario's wagon tracks, only to find that Vásquez had arrived two hours before and ridden off with her.

Leiva in custody willingly confessed, identified the gang members, and described who had killed each victim. The manhunt began again. Rosario, several months pregnant, suffered a miscarriage, but stayed with Vásquez for two months. Then, with proceeds from another robbery, Vásquez paid for her train fare home to stay with her family's friends. Sheriff Adams decided to pursue the other gang members, jailing and prosecuting one of Vásquez's cousins, and using Leiva's testimony to send the man to San Quentin. Rosario finally agreed to testify, too.

The hunt for Vásquez, the Tres Pinos murderer, continued, but the bandido remained elusive. He easily found recruits for a new Vásquez gang, and, on December 26, Vásquez struck again, at Kingston (near Layton) in Fresno County. His gang of ten to twelve desperadoes raided tills and robbed store employees, customers, and others. The entire town was ransacked. Thirty-five people had been tied up and robbed before the gang was chased out of town in a raging gunfight organized by a major rancher. Visalia, a Central Valley town, was raided on January 4, 1874. Vásquez's exploits ranged as far as the mines in the Eastern Sierra.

On January 2, Governor Booth had sent the reward request to California's legislature and appointed Harry Morse as the state's manhunter. Morse set off on his marathon ride to track down leads and capture Vásquez, alive or dead. Morse's posse, pretending to be a survey group or stock buyers, set off in March for a sixty-one day, 2,700-mile odyssey.

Vásquez decided to head to Los Angeles in April. He had given himself a title: captain, and said he was a defender of all Californians, all Mexicans. But, niece Felicita had had his baby and the family was very upset. Along the way, Vásquez stopped long enough to beg forgiveness of her father, his brother, Chico.

Vásquez stayed with Greek George, who had originally arrived in the United States as a camel driver when the army had tried a supply line using the animals. His wife was upset about Vásquez and Felicita's baby. A raid south of the San Gabriel Valley to rob a sheep rancher who had just sold a large flock yielded a check for $800. A teenage nephew was sent to downtown Los Angeles to cash it. The nephew was very nervous in the bank, and, with this clue, Sheriff Rowland's posse chased Vásquez's gang all over the hills around the sheep ranch they had robbed. The bandido left a saddle and gun behind on the trail, but he was nowhere to be found.

Morse's tip for Rowland could not have come at a better time. Rowland sent a deputy sheriff to stake out Greek George's. With confirmation, Rowland knew he couldn't be in the posse because Vásquez would recognize him. Under-sheriff Albert Johnson, the Los Angeles police chief, a city detective, a policeman, the deputy responsible for the stakeout, and *San Francisco Chronicle* reporter George Beers made up the posse.

They arrived about a mile above Greek George's on a foggy May morning. The fog lifted in the afternoon, and Johnson stopped two Mexicans in a wagon to ask where they were going. Wood delivery, they said. The wagon was appropriated, the posse members were hidden on the floorboard, and the Mexicans were ordered to drive to Greek George's adobe. Inside the adobe, the usual delivery wagon had been noticed. As they approached, the lawmen and reporter got out with guns ready.

It was lunchtime. Johnson and the city detective burst through the front door shooting. Vásquez jumped through the kitchen window. There, reporter Beers was waiting, and fired into the bandit's shoulder. The police chief fired his double-barreled gun loaded with buckshot at almost the same time. They ran after Vásquez who was wounded and standing with his teenage gang member by the adobe wall. Beers gave the outlaw first-aid, and then the bandits were loaded into a wagon for the long ride back to Los Angeles.

They had him! They had captured "Captain" Tiburcio Vásquez!

Beers was one of three reporters to whom Vásquez granted interviews. After a short time in the Los Angeles County Jail, the bandit was taken to San Jose for his January 1875 trial on the charge of murdering the Los Pinos hotel keeper. While in jail he read, autographed and sold photographs, greeted hundreds of visitors and well-wishers, and graciously accepted flowers from a constant stream of women.

The trial took four days. The jury took two hours to return with a first degree murder verdict. The sentence was death by hanging. Vásquez's clemency plea was denied by Governor Romualdo Pacheco, a man with *californio* heritage.

El Bandido calmly drank wine and smoked a cigar before he was led out to the scaffold where a head covering and noose were adjusted. When Tiburcio Vásquez was hanged on March 19, 1875, the only word the crowd heard was his: "Pronto."

SOURCES

Reporters wrote down every word Vásquez uttered during his final trial and conducted interviews during the bandido's last imprisonment. Several newspapermen, including the reporter who was present and shot Vásquez at his capture, immediately published their conversations. Vásquez's life has been fodder for many writers and for many who romanticize him as a handsome womanizer and *californio* Robin Hood. San Francisco attorney and writer of Western history, John Boesssenecker, set out to write the definitive Vásquez biography that would define the man's history and motives, in *Bandido: The Life and Times of Tiburcio Vasquez*

(Norman, Okla.: University of Oklahoma Press, 2010). Blow-by-blow descriptions of gunfights are graphic and riveting.

Agnus MacLean's grandfather was a local doctor who tended to upstanding citizens and bandits alike. Family members' and friends' stories recalled Vasquez's exploits, some more legendary than based in fact. Weaving historical facts about Vasquez with plausible events in a semi-fictionalized narrative, Agnus MacLean, in *Legends of the California Bandidos* (Fresno: Pioneer Publishing Co., 1977) brings the bandido to life. The late Fresno historian William Secrest wrote the "'I have always avoided bloodshed': The Dangerous Days of Tiburcio Vasquez" chapter for his book *California Desperadoes: Stories of Early California Outlaws in Their Own Words* (Fresno, Calif.: Quill Driver Books, 2000).

CHAPTER 7

Black Bart
Classy Robber of the Foothills

C alifornia bandidos came in many versions. Charles Earl Boles robbed his first stagecoach in 1875, driven by what may have been economic need or payback for some wrong or slight. Much written about him at the time was speculation about the highwayman's origins and background, his real identity, and his motive. Newspaper reporters put fear into the heart of the consuming public while throwing out occasional hints of liaisons with women, and even contriving to give him a Robin Hood "take from the rich to give to the poor" personality. Rather than a loaded gun, the real bandit's "weapon" was poetry left at the scene of a couple of his early stagecoach robberies. Black Bart, as he nicknamed himself, was notorious. His gentlemanly approach and bits of verse created an elegant legend from which writers have been trying to separate fact from fiction ever since he left recorded history in 1888. Black Bart was a criminal jerk, but a classy one.

> *I've labored long and hard for bread—*
> *For honor and for riches—*
> *But on my corns too long youve tred*
> *You fine haired sons of bitches.*
> *Black Bart*

> *Driver, give my respects to our friend, the other driver; but*
> *I really had a notion to hang my old disguise hat on his*
> *weather eye.*

The handwritten waybill found after the fact at the scene of the August 3, 1877, stagecoach robbery gave the man who was to become California's most famous bandit his name and identity. It was Black Bart's fourth of an eventual twenty-eight (or twenty-nine) robberies that made him distinctive among solo operator stage robbers in California: He became a man with a unique costume, a pen name, and a mysterious persona.

Black Bart had no gang to back him up. He was notably polite when he firmly told stagecoach drivers in a memorable bass voice, "Throw down the box!" The white flour sack with eyeholes that covered his head was better than a Zorro-style mask would have been at masking his real identity. The double-barreled shotgun the man in the well-worn linen duster wielded spoke volumes, although he never fired it.

Black Bart's human targets, stagecoach drivers, worked for Wells Fargo Express Company. Wells Fargo & Co. had opened an office on Montgomery Street in San Francisco in March 1852 to offer the Gold Rush mining camps a safe way for miners and merchants to ship gold, gold dust, and other valuables from point to point. A locked green treasure box made of pine, oak, and iron was carried under the stagecoach driver's seat. Drivers guided teams of four or six horses while sitting perched on a board in front of the body of the round-shaped passenger coach. Wells Fargo & Co.'s red stages with the company name in yellow-gold letters became a symbol of the West. In bad weather, cold, summer heat, and caked with dust or mud, the drivers' determination and skill were legendary. Even Mark Twain remarked on the cradle-like quality of the specially manufactured coaches' suspension as they moved at a pace of five or so miles per hour over rough terrain and mountains. Wells Fargo & Co.'s express shipments were transported along with sacks of United States mail stowed separately from the locked treasure box.

Rural communities, like many in the Mother Lode gold country of the Sierra Nevada foothills, depended on the stagecoaches' predictable schedules. Horses were changed at regular livery stables after each twelve miles. Rest and refreshment stops were made at home stations, often small hotels or roadhouses. A

Black Bart
PHOTO USED WITH PERMISSION FROM WELLS FARGO BANK, N.A.,
PROVIDED COURTESY SAN FRANCISCO HISTORY CENTER, SAN FRANCISCO PUBLIC LIBRARY

full complement of passengers, up to twelve people, could ride, although stages weren't always full. The valuables and mail went regardless.

Drivers would often have an armed man, a shotgun messenger literally riding [with a] shotgun sitting next to them for protection. Wells Fargo records note 347 robbery attempts on their stagecoaches from 1870 to 1884. Black Bart attempted twenty-eight or twenty-nine of those robberies (the number varies) between 1875–1883 in the Sierra Nevada foothills, Sonoma and Mendocino Counties, and far northern California, even venturing into southern Oregon.

Since the Gold Rush boom, gold production had been steadily declining through the 1850s and 1860s. Increasingly, the lock-boxes carried paper transactions, often in the form of checks. A road agent, or bandit such as Black Bart, had no guarantee that there would be anything in the box, that what was there was truly valuable, or that what he found could be sold or cashed without provoking suspicion. Once Wells Fargo declared company policy to be "never to abandon or relax the pursuit of anyone who committed a criminal offense," against it, it doggedly went after road agents. And Black Bart's audacity and numerous forced stagecoach halts made him a major candidate for apprehension by Wells Fargo & Co.

The company's chief enforcer and lawman, James B. Hume, was the head of the Special Agent division. A New Yorker, Hume had arrived with Gold Rush prospectors in 1849 and stayed to become tax collector, city marshal, police chief, and the El Dorado County sheriff. As sheriff, Hume methodically tracked down stagecoach robbers using detective techniques that were rare in the era, such as comparing bullets and weapons. He accepted Wells Fargo's offer to continue his work as its chief detective in 1872.

Every good guy like Hume needs a nemesis. Enter Black Bart, stagecoach robber, sometime poet, leading multiple lives in rural parts of northern California and urban San Francisco. When the highwayman who would later be known as Black Bart got away with his first robbery on Funk Hill, east of Copperopolis in Cala-veras County on July 26, 1875, Wells Fargo took note as it did of any stage robbery.

This robber, with a flour sack head covering often supple-mented with a hat, his double-barreled shotgun, and polite man-ner, was smart enough to keep one of the valuable team horses between himself and the driver and shotgun messenger. Though the drivers sometimes organized posses or searchers to go back and track this robber, many of them remarked on a politeness that was almost chivalrous. Black Bart once returned a lady's purse, thrown out of the carriage, unopened. No one inside a coach was ever threatened or attacked. In fact, it began to get noticed that this robber didn't use actual violence or force, merely seriously threatened it with the business end of a shotgun.

No one ever saw a getaway horse. Searchers and organized posses, both local authorities and those sent by Wells Fargo, would find that this robber axed open the treasure box near the scene of the crime, sliced the mail bags open with a unique T-shaped slit, and often scattered open envelopes about before he fled with whatever loot there was. His tracks always petered out. This man seemed to be good at getting across country, sometimes walk-ing twenty-five miles per day, without leaving campfire traces or other evidence. Mountains posed no barrier to his movements. Black Bart's progress was meticulously noted by Wells Fargo's chief detective, Hume, every time there was another Bart-style robbery reported, even if it happened in an area far-distant from his last appearance.

Occasionally, Black Bart returned to the locale of a prior rob-bery. Once, investigators found that the robber had been eating apples while waiting for the stagecoach to come into view. Another time, investigators found evidence of peach-eating. The axes used to get the treasure boxes opened were often taken from nearby, then discarded.

For whatever reason, two years after beginning his career, Black Bart left his first poem on a waybill not far from his fourth stage robbery site south of Fort Ross in Sonoma County. On July, 25, 1878, after his fifth robbery of the Quincy to Oroville stage, another poem was found in the express box:

Here I lay me down to sleep
to wait the coming morrow
perhaps success perhaps defeat
and everlasting sorrow.
Let come what will, I'll try it on,
My condition can't be worse.
But if there's money in the box
It's munny in my purse.
Black Bart the Po8

Both had been written in a different handwriting for each line, perhaps another way to confuse any lawman on his trail. Who was Black Bart, a man who may have taken his moniker from a bad character in a sequel to *The Case of Summerfield,* a book also serialized in the day's newspapers, where the plot thickens as a mad scientist bent on destroying the world is foiled?

Black Bart's deliberate efforts to deny or to be vague about his background make his origins and activities prior to arrival in California somewhat sketchy. Charles Earl Bowles was probably born in England and immigrated as a baby with his family to Jefferson County, New York, in 1830. At some point, his last name changed to Boles. Charles felt the lure of the California Gold Rush and spent most of four years over two trips mining and prospecting not very successfully in the Mother Lode counties he would eventually traverse as Black Bart. He returned to New York and married Mary Elizabeth Johnson in about 1856. Daughters were born in Iowa in 1857, in New York in 1859, and near Decatur, Illinois, in 1861. There are no records of Charles Boles's work, trade, or profession.

In the US Civil War, he enlisted in 1862 as a private in Company B of the Illinois Volunteer Infantry, and during three years of fighting, Boles was in seventeen major battles, was wounded three times, and received a 1st Lieutenant battlefield commission.

After the war, he returned to Iowa, to his wife and children. He may have had a son. By May 1, 1867, Boles had departed for a mining camp near Butte, Montana. Except for a letter to his wife, Mary, in 1871 saying that he would return with a stake (mining proceeds), Boles probably didn't have much luck in Montana. After that letter, Charles Boles effectively cut his ties—there were no letters to Mary for twelve years—and disappeared.
Where had Boles gone and why?

Enter Charles E. Bolton, a mild-mannered, blue-eyed, five-foot-eight-inch man with gray to whitish hair and a mustache. This gentleman of indeterminate middle age who dressed well sported a decorous diamond pin in his tie. Those who noted Bolton's presence in San Francisco from about 1875 to 1883 thought he had mining interests somewhere never specified in northern California that required frequent trips to keep up with business. Most of his travels were in the better summer weather season extending into fall. Unusual for a man of the time, Bolton didn't smoke or drink, although he may have invested in mining stocks and played an occasional game of poker. Usually, Mr. Bolton, though friendly, kept to himself, was liked by rooming house hostesses for his gracious manners, and was noted as a good listener rather than saying much himself.

Eventually, Wells Fargo & Co., began locking the express box onto the inside of the stagecoach. That complicated matters for highwaymen who were forced to order any passengers out to be able to get to the box. If, like Black Bart, they were acting without accomplices, the robber would have to keep an eye on the driver, shotgun messenger, and passengers. The solutions were either to order them all to walk down the road far enough away to not allow a sniper shot, or to enlist the help of the protesting driver. Black Bart's gun emphasized that he meant business, and the experienced stagecoach drivers knew their priorities were to deliver the contents of the treasure box, express box, mail sacks, and any passengers to the destination. Once, Bart called over his shoulder to his other "boys," in actuality sticks placed in nearby vegetation to look like guns.

Wells Fargo Chief Detective Hume would send "Wanted" posters to company agents, alerting them to recent activity and sometimes offering a reward. Recipients were warned not to post the notices, but "to place these Circulars in the hands of Officers and discreet persons only." There was a standing reward for the arrest and conviction of stage robbers. For Black Bart, Hume's reward offer was $800, including $300 from Wells Fargo; $300 authorized by California Governor William Irwin; and $200 from the federal Postal Department for a mail-robbery conviction. Eventually, Hume's notices offered one-quarter of the amount recovered from a robber's take as an additional reward incentive.

The chase was on. It would take a clue and good detective work to find Black Bart.

What would turn out to be Black Bart's last robbery on November 3, 1883, targeted the often-robbed Sonora to Milton stage driven by Reason E. McConnell. It was the same hill and location as Black Bart's first robbery eight years before in 1875. Before dawn, McConnell had picked up and secured an express box with 228 ounces of (gold) amalgam, $550 in gold coins, and several ounces of gold dust. He had breakfast, changed horses, and took Jimmy Rolleri, the son of the owner of the hotel at Reynolds Ferry, to ride a short way beside the driver until he dropped Rolleri off with his gun to hunt deer around Funk Hill. McConnell would head on to Copperopolis.

Rolleri was dropped off and began walking downhill. McConnell had almost reached the top of Funk Hill when Black Bart emerged and demanded to know where the other man had gone. Told the extra man was gone, the robber told McConnell to get down, but McConnell tried to resist, telling a lie that the stagecoach brake wasn't working. Instead of ordering McConnell to turn the coach around to a point where it wouldn't be pulled backward or slide, Bart told McConnell to block the wheel with a rock and when McConnell refused, did so himself. Then he ordered the driver to unhitch the horses and lead them away. Bart took an axe to the box. A short distance away from the robber, McConnell was then able to signal Rolleri to move unseen around Bart's position, and they met up. One of them, probably Rolleri (who was later rewarded by Wells Fargo with a fine gun inscribed with the date), fired a shot that hit Black Bart's hand. The highwayman quickly disappeared into the bushes.

McConnell hitched his team and dashed to telegraph the Calaveras County Sheriff, Ben Thorn, and Hume's office in San Francisco. Local men, including Rolleri, joined a local Wells Fargo agent and raced to see where Black Bart may have gone. Hours later as it began to get dark, they found Bart's previous night's campsite behind a rock. There were grocery bags, head-covering flour sacks, an opera glasses case, a magnifying glass, some linen cuffs, a razor, and a belt. In his office later, Sheriff Thorn contemplated one other thing—buckshot tied up inside a grungy handkerchief. The local Wells Fargo agent noticed the faint laundry mark, F.X.0.7., on the silk cloth.

On November 5, Hume issued another notice about the latest Sonora to Milton stage robbery, noting a "LIBERAL REWARD."

Harry N. Morse, who had previously been both sheriff of Alameda County and the head of a state-authorized posse to hunt down bandido Tiburcio Vásquez in 1874, had been engaged by Hume in summer 1883 for a private investigation of the proliferating Black Bart robberies. Morse may, as he later claimed, be the one who connected the mark with the correct laundry establishment among ninety-one in San Francisco. Eventually, the laundry was identified, and by pretending to be interested in meeting the mining gentleman who belonged to the laundry mark, Morse came up with a C. E. Bolton.

Meanwhile, Black Bart had walked to Sacramento, washed and changed into good clothes, then taken the train to Reno, Nevada, for a few days before returning to San Francisco. He had notified his landlady and a friend who handled the laundry service that he'd be returning. Morse's probe had led him to that friend, T. C. Ware, who introduced Morse (who said his name was Hamilton) to Bolton when the well-dressed gentleman passed them on the street. Morse told Bolton that he had some mining to discuss and ores to show him. He took Bolton's arm as they walked down the street. Suddenly Morse steered them through the Wells Fargo & Co. office doors on Montgomery Street and beyond into Hume's office. Bolton, who insisted he was Bolton and owned a mine somewhere on the California-Nevada state line, was persistently asked his whereabouts for November 1 through 5. San Francisco Police Captain Appleton Stone arrived. Bolton was offered a choice of revealing his whereabouts or being locked up in the city jail. He chose the jail.

Hume, Morse, Stone, and "Bolton" first went to Bolton's boarding house, and his room, valises, and belongings were examined. Clothing matching the Black Bart descriptions was found, along with the same laundry mark on some items, and a Bible that had been presented to Charles E. Boles. He was arrested and taken back to the city jail.

To make a case against Bolton/Boles as Black Bart, eyewitnesses had to identify the robber and place him at the scene or in the area where the crime was committed at the correct time. Witnesses did not travel to San Francisco; the San Francisco County lawman, Captain Stone, accompanied by private investigator Morse, would take the suspect back to Calaveras County where an alerted Sheriff Thorn had a warrant sworn out. In Milton, Reason McConnell identified Black Bart from his voice.

Thorn; Morse; Hume's assistant, John Thacker; and Bolton rode in a buckboard to San Andreas and the Calaveras County Jail. Bolton's questioning began after the investigators had finished dinner. After almost five hours and Morse's constant reminder that there would be a trial soon, Bolton is quoted as asking, "Mind you, I do not admit that I committed this robbery. But what benefit would it be to the man who did acknowledge it?"

As with everything swirling about Black Bart, which man got him to admit to the recent Funk Hill robbery with a hint or suggestion that confessing to one robbery would get him a shorter sentence than being tried and convicted of many robberies, is in doubt. His captors would have been eligible for the reward for a portion of recovered stolen goods. About 12:30 a.m., Bolton told Morse and Sheriffs Stone and Thorn, "Well, let's go after it,"— referring to his hold-up take.

Under moonlight during a twenty-mile carriage ride back to Funk Hill, Black Bart started his confession to the lawmen, although he refused to *be* anyone but Charles Bolton. He had been acquainted with many San Francisco policemen, and he said he hadn't been worried because he'd only associated with good people and no one knew what he really did. Finally, Black Bart showed them the log under which he'd stashed the recent loot: amalgam, gold coins, and gold dust.

Back in San Andreas with the goods recovered, Sheriff Thorn locked Bolton up in jail. Two days later, still denying that he was Black Bart, Charles E. Bolton pleaded guilty to only the latest, November 3, robbery as a first offense, and waived a jury trial. Perhaps because of his eagerness to confess to one robbery and to help recover what he stole, as well as California's and Wells Fargo's desire to get Black Bart out of commission, the judge only considered the single robbery. Bolton's sentence was six years in prison.

First, Bolton spent a night back in the San Francisco jail, greeting friends, acquaintances, policemen, and holding forth humorously for the newspapermen. He never admitted to being anyone but Bolton, nor to more than the one robbery to which he had confessed. He adamantly denied being Black Bart.

Finally Sheriff Thorn and Bolton took the ferry to Marin County. Charles E. Bolton entered San Quentin on November 21, 1883, eighteen days after Black Bart committed his final robbery. Upon his incarceration for the crime of robbery, San Quentin Prisoner #11046 listed his occupation as "mining" and said that he was fifty years old. His place of birth was Jefferson County, New York. His education was "liberal," and he didn't smoke, drink, or take opium. His vital details were spare, but generally matched what people had thought they had noticed about Black Bart: five feet eight inches tall, 160 pounds, a light complexion, a nearly white mustache and imperial (upward curling whiskers on his upper lip and cheeks), and a number 6 shoe size.

On November 26, Hume sent a notice to Wells Fargo & Co. agents that since the conviction and incarceration of Charles E. Boles, alias Charles E. Bolton, alias "Black Bart, the Po8," he had received law officer questions about whether the man was actually Black Bart. To quell the queries, lower on the notice, Hume placed the San Quentin admission description and a recent photograph of "B.B."

With the name of "Charles E. Boles" in Bolton's San Francisco boarding house room Bible, a San Francisco newspaper was able to find his wife, Mary Boles, then living with a daughter in Hannibal, Missouri. While in San Quentin, Bolton/Boles corresponded back and forth with Mary, promising a reunion in vague terms. He wrote at least one daughter, a brother, and other relatives, although his family members later burned many letters.

California's Goodwin Act provided a formula for time off for good behavior, and Bolton was released on January 21, 1888, after serving four years and two months. Dressed as well as he had been when he was arrested, Bolton arrived in San Francisco at the Ferry Building and spoke to reporters. One asked if he would resume his career as a highwayman to which Bolton/Boles/Black Bart emphatically replied, "No!" Another asked if he'd write poetry? "Young man, didn't you hear me say I would commit no more crimes?" the Po8 replied, to laughter.

He rented a room at Nevada House on Sixth Street, and soon wrote to Mary Boles that he must disappoint his family, that it was "utterly impossible" to return. He wrote her two more letters, then left San Francisco and was last known to have registered under yet another name at a Visalia Hotel. When he departed, leaving a valise in the hotel owner's care, Charles E. Bolton, or Charles E. Boles, or Black Bart vanished forever. The valise was sent to Hume, and inside he found cuffs with the telltale laundry mark, neckties, coffee, canned meats, sugar, pickles, and incongruously, a jar of currant jelly.

For most of the next twenty years, there were regular reports of Black Bart sightings around the world. James B. Hume, who served as Wells Fargo & Co.'s chief detective for thirty years until his death in 1904, always denied that Black Bart had come back. Black Bart, the Po8, was, after all, no longer wanted for any crime against Wells Fargo & Co.

Sources

Of all the bad guys to grace California in the post–Gold Rush period, no one rivals Black Bart with the telling of varying versions of his history and life. Too much is missing in documents for a boring chronological biography, so the details of the place and circumstances of each robbery, most of the bare-bones narrative of Bart's confession, and some facts about his incarceration in and correspondence from San Quentin are always the only solid base for books and stories about the gentleman bandit.

Bart gets a chapter, "The Poetical Career of Black Bart" in Alvin F. Harlow's *Old Waybills: The Romance of the Express Companies* (New York: D. Appleton-Century Company, Inc., 1934), where he's described as the "mildest, most gentle and harmless bandit who ever looked through a gunsight." Joseph Henry Jackson's *Bad Company* (Lincoln: University of Nebraska Press, 1939) covers "The Story of California's Legendary and Actual Stage-Robbers, Bandits, Highwaymen and Outlaws from the Fifties to the Eighties," including Black Bart, in well-written narrative that clearly points to the newspapers' adding facts to make Bart's background interesting and plausible.

In *Black Bart: The True Story of The West's Most Famous Stagecoach Robber* (Mendocino, Calif.: Pacific Transcriptions, 1992), William Collins and Bruce Levene went back to reconstruct the highwayman's life, researched with enormous detail. Appendices add speculative and spurious stories, tales of Black Bart's purported love life, a lengthy "interview" printed after he disappeared (!) in the December 2, 1888, *San Francisco Examiner,* bogus poems, and other apocrypha that "confirm" the embellished lore surrounding the robber.

Black Bart: Boulevardier Bandit, by George Hoeper (Fresno, Calif.: Word Dancer Press, 1995), evokes the rural countryside in which Black Bart carried out his stage robberies, and, as with the other books, lists and disposes of speculation about Bart's after-release activities and whereabouts. The Wells Fargo & Company website includes a history section, found at www.wellsfargohistory.com.

CHAPTER 8

Rabble-Rousing Racist
Dennis Kearney Crusades against the Chinese

Racists are a particularly nasty type of jerk.

No one was a more virulent spokesperson for anti-Chinese sentiment than the Irish-born leader of San Francisco's Workingmen's Party, Dennis Kearney. In the late 1870s, his rabble-rousing and railing against the Chinese led to passage of the Chinese Exclusion Act of 1882. Not all jerks get "caught." Some just give their name to a movement: Dennis Kearney and Kearneyism came to define a particularly vicious version of badness.

The Chinese must go!

Dennis Kearney's slogan was short, clear, and brutal. On vacant sandlots near City Hall in San Francisco's Civic Center, Kearney's true believers gathered to hear him speak in late 1877. Workingmen, the economically disgruntled, and Chinese haters assembled to hear the Irishman's harangues against the most foreign, the most different-looking arrivals in California—the Chinese. Every Kearney oration began and ended with, "The Chinese must go!" and brought a roar from the crowd.

Dennis Kearney was born in 1847 in County Cork, Ireland, and so had not seen the original Chinese arrivals who, like other prospectors, headed off quickly from San Francisco, *Dabu* ("First City") to the Gold County interior of *Jinshan* ("Gold Mountain"), California. Less than one hundred Chinese lived in California before that 1849 Gold Rush. By 1850, four thousand had arrived, and Chinese prospectors were beginning to get pushed out of mining camps. Finally, the Chinese miners were reduced to going through the tailings, the rubble left as worthless by others. Yet, the Chinese did find gold in the tailings, spurring more resentment for their tenacity and hard work. Some Chinese left the mines and set up small service businesses, especially general stores, laundries, and restaurants; "owned" shoe-making and cigar-manufacturing industries; worked on farms; or became household servants. Their wages were often as low as one dollar a day for many hours of work. By the time Kearney whipped up anti-Chinese frenzy in 1877, there were 116,000 Chinese, mostly men, in California.

How did a man with a brogue, an immigrant himself, come to this moment of demagoguery?

Kearney had gone to sea in the merchant marine and arrived in San Francisco as first officer of a clipper ship in 1868. For the next few years, he sailed the California coast on a steamship. Twenty-five years old and ready to marry and settle down in San Francisco, in 1872, Kearney became a naturalized citizen and bought a drayage business that prospered with three open-sided wagons hauling freight for short distances. He claimed to be a self-taught and self-made man, and was proud of speaking at Sunday meetings of the Lyceum for Self-Culture.

While Kearney was growing up and at sea, the boomtown atmosphere of 1850s San Francisco had been bolstered by the Comstock Lode silver discovery near Virginia City, Nevada, in the late 1850s and early 1860s. Four one-time Sacramento merchants and businessmen, associates later known as The Big Four, had incorporated the Central Pacific Railroad and built it over the Sierra Nevada to meet the Union Pacific Railroad in Promontory, Utah, in 1869. The western part of that Transcontinental Railroad had been built by laborers from many places, including Ireland and China. Charles Crocker, one of The Big Four (Crocker, Leland Stanford, Mark Hopkins, Collis Huntington), had contracted for Chinese labor at extremely low wages to build the railway and frequently expressed satisfaction with the good and hard work done by "his" Chinese workers.

No one had expected the good times to falter. As the 1870s began, the Irish, Chinese, and others no longer had railroad construction work and drifted toward cities. US immigration, especially from Europe, was increasing dramatically. Plagues of locusts descended on and decimated crops during the severe drought years from 1870 to 1877. In 1873, the temporary ten-day closure of the New York Stock Exchange, triggered by a major banker unable to secure funding for railroads, started an economic depression that spread across the country. In 1875, the prestigious Bank of California failed, and its main owner, William Ralston, who had profited from the Comstock Lode, walked into San Francisco Bay to his death, a possible suicide. By 1877, the unemployed and homeless felt disenfranchised, ready to strike out at any perceived threat.

The Chinese presented an obvious target. In San Francisco, as in other towns in California and the West, Chinese immigrants had gathered together in enclaves, Chinatowns. Language and culture were familiar, people of the same clan and region of China could be together, and there might be some protection from frequent outsiders' attacks. Men wore tunics and loose pants and a single braid, or queue. The queue had been an imperial Chinese mandate for centuries. In a direct move against the Chinese, San Francisco passed the Queue Ordinance in 1873 that required that any prisoner have his hair cut to one inch, a condition that culturally shamed and cut any Chinese man off from his heritage. Whites demeaned Chinese by calling them "coolies," "Mongolians," or "John Chinaman."

The Queue Ordinance, though vetoed by the mayor and later overturned by the courts, was among many measures in California—and San Francisco—that discriminated against the Chinese. Most, but not all, were challenged, and some were repealed or ruled unconstitutional. Among them was a tax on non-citizens arriving on a ship (1855–1857); a Chinese Fisherman's (monthly) Tax (1860–1864); and a Chinese Police Tax levying a fee against "Mongolians" (1862–1863), that was universally called California's Anti-Coolie Tax. In 1854, the US Supreme Court had held that testimony by Chinese was inadmissible in court.

Dennis Kearney speaking to the workers at a meeting in October 1877
COURTESY SAN FRANCISCO HISTORY CENTER, SAN FRANCISCO PUBLIC LIBRARY.
ILLUSTRATION BY G. W. PETERS FOR *SCRIBNER'S*, OCTOBER 1895.

For San Francisco Chinese living in close quarters in their Chinatown, the 1870s brought several particularly severe local laws. The Cubic Air Ordinance in 1870 required that any room rental have five hundred cubic feet of air per person. That same year, citizens were not allowed to carry loads on across-the-shoulder poles under provisions of the Sidewalk Ordinance, when the only people who did so were the Chinese.

At first, Kearney wasn't after the Chinese. Businessman Dennis Kearney started to use his voice to express his opinions, at first disparaging all workers as lazy, despicable drinkers and implying that self-made men like him were hard-working. It was 1877, and a railroad strike that had begun on July 14, in Martinsburg, West Virginia, would spread to Maryland, Pennsylvania, and Illinois that summer. San Francisco's sandlot gatherings were restive with dissatisfaction that had spread west from the strikes, and speakers addressed massed assemblies with passion.

The socialist Workingman's Party of the United States called a sandlot meeting for July 23, a Monday, at 7:00 p.m. San Francisco was tense and several people had been arrested for displaying banners about the meeting that was being organized, after all, by the reorganized International Workingmen's Association originally started by Karl Marx.

The mob came primed with resentment against the rich. That rich man, Crocker, who lived with the other highfalutin nabobs, mostly railroad barons, on Nob Hill, had imported all those Chinese to work on the railroad years before. In addition, there were all those recent arrivals from China who disembarked in Mission Bay at the Pacific Mail Steamship Docks to take jobs at low wages. The usual anger against rich profiteers and sympathy with the railroad strikers were expressed by the speakers.

No one mentioned the Chinese that night, but they were not far away from anyone's mind. Something, perhaps a gunshot, neighborhood toughs, or the beating of a Chinese man, created a disturbance that riled the eight thousand edgy people rallied on the sandlot.

A group peeled away and headed for Chinatown. In the darkness, twenty Chinese laundries were ruined, and the Chinese Methodist Mission building had been attacked. Hoodlums were blamed for the riot as police and volunteers spent several days chasing and battling the perpetrators through the streets. Harking back to Committee of Vigilance days, by Wednesday, a four-thousand-man-strong Pickhandle Brigade had been deputized by the resurrected Committee of Public Safety to keep order. The armed brigade kept rioters from burning the Pacific Mail Steamship docks when a ship carrying Chinese immigrants arrived on schedule. Kearney was a Brigader, wielding a pickaxe handle, a wooden baton that was effective in close quarters. The docks survived, but there were fires and rioting elsewhere in the city. By the end of July, there were four dead and fourteen wounded men.

Kearney always claimed that the riot galvanized him, that he had seen the power of the workingman. What he never explained was why, within a month of the riot, he had organized a political party for the workers and suddenly begun to loudly condemn both the Chinese and the capitalists who he said exploited the workers and hired the Chinese.

He applied, but was denied membership by the Workingmen's Party of the United States that probably wondered why this harsh critic of workers wanted to associate with those he had called lazy the month before. Kearney needed a power base. By August, he was secretary of the Workingmen's Trade and Labor Union. In September, Kearny shouted to swelling sandlot crowds that twenty thousand men with arms could take down the rich capitalists. By October, Kearney had established his own Workingmen's Party of California. The phrase he added to each speech became Kearney's distinctive signature rant, "The Chinese must go!"

President Kearney and Secretary H. L. Knight of the Workingmen's Party of California wrote a letter, a manifesto, published by the *San Francisco Chronicle* editor on October 16:

We have made no secret of our intentions. We make none. Before you and before the world we declare that the China-man must leave our shores. We declare that white men, and women, and boys, and girls, cannot live as the people of the great republic should and compete with the single Chinese coolie in the labor market. We declare that we cannot hope to drive the Chinaman away by working cheaper than he does. None but an enemy would expect it of us; none but an idiot could hope for success; none but a degraded coward and slave would make the effort. To an American, death is preferable to life on a par with the Chinaman.

It continues, denouncing land grabbers, bloated bondholders, railroad magnates, shoddy aristocrats, and the legislature for being bribed by the rich. It went on,

"Treason is better than to labor beside a Chinese slave."

Everyone in town would have read these fighting words in the newspaper, so when the sandlot gathering on October 29 reached its daily moment of drama, Kearney and three thousand followers marched quickly to and up Nob Hill and stood massed in front of the (Charles) Crocker Mansion. Kearney's words were reported later, on November 5, in the *San Francisco Evening Bulletin,* two days after he had been arrested on November 3 for inciting his followers to violence—or at least disturbing the peace—with this speech:

The Central Pacific men are thieves, and will soon feel the power of the workingmen. When I have thoroughly orga-nized my party, we will march through the city and compel the thieves to give up their plunder. I will lead you to the city hall, clear out the police force, hang the prosecuting attorney, burn every book that has a particle of law in it, and then enact new laws for the workingmen. I will give the Central Pacific just three months to discharge their

*Chinamen, and if that is not done Stanford and his crowd
will have to take the consequences. I will give Crocker until
November 29th to take down the fence around Yung's house*
[called the spite fence that Crocker built when a neighbor
wouldn't sell his land], *and if he does not do it, I will lead
the workingmen up there and tear it down, and give Crocker
the worst beating with the sticks that a man ever got.*

After Kearney's arrest, Chinatown leaders worried about repri-
sals by Kearney's followers. Those leaders were collectively known
in English as the Chinese Six Companies. The "companies" (*hui-
guan* or *hui-kuan*) were benevolent associations that took care of
the affairs of Chinese from a specific region in China. They helped
new arrivals, provided transportation home, prepared remains for
shipment to China to be buried in home village soil, mediated disputes, and as a group, provided a unified front to non-Chinese.

The Chinese Six Companies wrote to warn San Francisco
Mayor Andrew Jackson Bryant:

*Large gatherings of the idle and irresponsible element of
the population of this city are nightly addressed in the open
streets by speakers who use the most violent, inflammatory,
and incendiary language, threatening in plainest terms to
burn and pillage the Chinese quarter and kill our people
unless, at their bidding, we leave this "free republic." The
continuance of these things for many days with increasing
fury, without any check or hinderance by the authorities,
is causing the Chinese people great anxiety, ...and should
a riotous attack be made upon the Chinese quarter, we
should have neither the power nor disposition to restrain
our countrymen from defending themselves to the last
extremity and selling their lives as dearly as possible.*

Their fear was warranted. In October 1871, in Los Angeles,
seventeen Chinese had been strung up in the night, lynched, and

several more were mutilated. A couple of corpses were slashed with knives. Looting of Chinese homes and businesses followed. In 1876, the Chinatown in Oroville in northern California was burned down. John Bidwell, who had founded Chico in 1860, and along with Leland Stanford, had a prosperous agricultural rancho worked by Chinese, supported his Chinese workers. But in 1876–1877, even though the Chinese were vigilant and often armed, whites who wanted their farm jobs but not the low wages burned buildings and brutally murdered Chinese in and near Rancho Chico. In San Francisco's confined urban setting, with tempers flaring, leaders knew anything could happen.

Other party leaders were arrested and joined Kearney in jail. Those remaining on the outside told the sandlot crowd that holding Kearney violated his—and their—constitutional right to free speech. On October 21, Kearney's case was tried and dismissed. Ten thousand people marched in a Thanksgiving Day parade in November to listen to Kearney and the other party men declaim against the perceived evils, specifically adding the railroad owners to the list of abusers of the workingman.

As 1878 dawned, the speeches continued, and Kearney was arrested multiple times on charges of conspiracy, inciting riots, and incendiary language. He was always acquitted by the juries. City residents, San Francisco city officials, and others began quietly organizing to defend themselves and city funds if Kearney and the Workingmen's Party managed to trigger a riot. Workingmen's Party members organized into military companies armed with rifles. Igniting Chinatown and sabotaging Pacific Mail Company steamships were mentioned publicly. A hangman's noose appeared.

Everyone, including the newspaper editors breathlessly reporting or enhancing each speech and detail, got the message. The board of supervisors immediately approved a penal code provision, passed by the state legislature in Sacramento and proclaimed by Mayor Bryant, that would jail anyone using violent language when speaking at meetings of twenty-five or more citizens—a gag order. Kearney and associates were on notice.

In this atmosphere, the Workingmen's Party of California convention meeting in San Francisco began on January 21, with Kearney as president and a party platform that addressed the Chinese issue:

> *Sec. 2 Chinese cheap labor is a curse to our land, a menace to our liberties and the institutions of our country, and should, therefore, be restricted and forever abolished.*

That spring, with the other parties talking about a new state constitution and a state convention to consider it, in April, Kearney had a falling out with the Workingmen's Party state committee. Within a few weeks, Kearney was ousted from the committee and from the party presidency on charges of corruption and abusing the party's resources.

In May, two rival Workingmen's Party conventions were held, and Kearney's faction garnered the majority of support. His group's platform bluntly demanded:

> *19. The Chinese laborer is a curse to our land, is degrading to our morals, is a menace to our liberties, and should be restricted and forever abolished, and "the Chinese must go."*
> *20. The employment of Chinese laborers by corporations formed under the laws of this state should be prohibited by law.*

The Workingmen's Party contributed about one-third of the delegates to California's Second Constitutional Convention. The party garnered state assembly seats in 1879. It even got the charismatic Reverend Isaac Kalloch elected as San Francisco mayor, after *San Francisco Chronicle* publisher Charles De Young shot candidate Kalloch ten days before the election. De Young was jailed while an injured Kalloch was kept under wraps until it was announced that he and the Workingmen's Party had handily won the election. The following April, Kalloch's son shot De Young to death.

By the time of that revenge murder, Mayor Kalloch, elected with such high hopes, wasn't meeting expectations. Perhaps the electorate had forgotten that the Baptist minister had once praised Chinese household workers from the pulpit and urged tolerance, but, in an about-face, quickly took up Kearney's refrains of "The Chinese must go" when the Workingmen's Party sought his support.

By 1880, Kearney's local popularity was waning as fellow party members fought with him and decided that his power had gone to his head—and perhaps to line his pockets with cash. San Franciscans were tired of the endless threats of violence and the feeling of an armed camp. Kearney departed the Workingmen's Party in a huff and drifted through membership in several other minor parties.

Nationally, Kearney had given his name to anti-Chinese racism and bigotry as Kearneyism. Cartoonists had a field day depicting Kearney versus the Chinese. One illustrator showed him as the "Peerless Wringer," shoving a Chinese man, bottom first, into a wringer over a washtub. The March 20, 1880, "Ides of March" cover of *Harper's Weekly* by the famous cartoonist Thomas Nast, shows laughing Chinese standing behind Kearney. Signs indicate that the orator is in the play *Julius Caesar* in the Sand-Lot Theatre. Kearney as the character Brutus is wearing a billboard that mentions the streets of San Francisco and other cities running with blood while pleading to "Kill me," as a sacrifice.

Anti-Chinese sentiment was growing. The US Congress passed the Chinese Exclusion Act of 1882, suspending immigration of laborers from China for ten years. The Scott Act of 1888 banned the return of Chinese laborers who had left the United States. More restrictive legislation was enacted over the years as the ten-year period in the Chinese Exclusion Act stretched for decades. It was expediently repealed in 1943 by the Magnuson Act when China was a US World War II ally.

And Kearney? Kearney's racist jerkiness never caught up with him. The demagogue had faded from the scene and from California politics by 1884. He toured the United States to urge passage of the Scott Act, and then did the same in Canada. Finally, his name disappeared from the papers. People heard that he had come into an inheritance in the 1890s. It was said that he made his peace with and may even have become friends with Charles Crocker. Before he died in near-obscurity in 1907, Kearney had become a prosperous Central Valley wheat farmer—one of the rich men he had once railed against.

POSTSCRIPT

In 2010, Chinese American history in California began a new chapter: Jean Quan, a Chinese-American woman whose forefathers were forced by the Exclusion Act to return to China to find wives, was elected mayor of Oakland. In January 2011, San Francisco City Administrator Edwin "Ed" M. Lee, a Chinese American, was appointed interim mayor in the city where 31 percent, nearly one-third of the population, was Asian-American..

SOURCES

Dennis Kearney is usually considered in the context of his comments and actions against the Chinese and for organizing the Workingmen's Party of California. The Workingmen's Party of California pamphlet denouncing the Chinese, local and state governments, and the press, *The Labor Agitators or The Battle for Bread* (San Francisco: Geo. W. Green, 1879) can be read online (digital id: cubcic brk5056) at the repository website for the Bancroft Library, University of California, Berkeley [xF870.C5 C51 v.2:4]. The Virtual Museum of San Francisco has an online collection of contemporaneous writings and photographs about the Chinese in the city (www.sfmuseum.net/hist1/index0.html#chinese).

In *Driven Out: The Forgotten War Aagainst Chinese Americans* (New York: Random House, 2007), University of Maryland professor of English, East Asian Studies, and Women's Studies, Jean Pfaelzer, comprehensively describes the discrimination against Chinese in the United States from the Gold Rush to nearly one hundred years later, the laws designed to keep Chinese immigrants out, and the legal battles to correct the injustice. Much of the book describes violent incidents including burning of Chinatowns throughout the western states, with particularly horrifying accounts of California's sins. A legal view of discrimination against Chinese in California and their legal actions to fight back with well-prepared legal cases is described in Boalt School of Law, University of California, Berkeley professor Charles J. McClain's book, *In Search of Equality: The Chinese Struggle against Discrimination in Nineteenth-Century America* (Berkeley: University of California Press, 1994). *Chinese San Francisco: 1850–1943,* by Yong Chen (Stanford, Calif.: Stanford University Press, 2000), explains what conditions in China existed when its citizens emigrated to California and social conditions and attitudes among arrivals who attempted to settle in the state.

In *Endangered Dreams: The Great Depression in California* (New York: Oxford University Press, 1997), historian Kevin Starr begins with a chapter, "The Left Side of The Continent: Radicalism in Nineteenth-Century San Francisco," that describes the 1870s economic downturn and anti-Chinese sentiment. And, in 1893, the California State Library arranged to publish Winfield J. Davis's *History of Political Conventions in California, 1849–1892,* which covered the 1877 rise of Kearneyism in San Francisco through contemporary statements, writing, and newspaper reports.

CHAPTER 9

Shoot-Out at Mussel Slough

Settlers, Land, and the Power of the Southern Pacific Railroad

The Mussel Slough incident, or "tragedy," in California's Central Valley, is classic Big Guys versus Little Guys. Envy automatically places blame on the rich and successful, like the four men who built and controlled the Central Pacific and Southern Pacific Railroads. The Big Four, as they were known, parlayed Gold Rush–era mercantile backgrounds in Sacramento and later in San Francisco into a transportation empire whose 1869 masterpiece was the western section of the Transcontinental Railroad.

Control of California politics, bribes, expert legal representation, and dominance in California transportation and land development created a reputation of a less than admirable corporate citizen that continued well into the twentieth century for Southern Pacific (SP). SP was often called The Octopus for its enterprises that reached far beyond its tracks carrying freight and passengers. Its public image was that of a corporate jerk, out to get the best of competitors and the little guy.

What might have been a local land dispute elsewhere in the West became a national story when SP appeared to be taking land from legal or squatting homesteaders who intended to or were cultivating land on or adjacent to the railway track right of way granted by the US government. Various and varying accounts of a shoot-out at Mussel Slough transformed a tragic event on May 11, 1880, into melodrama. What happened at Mussel Slough affected land use laws and contributed to formal interstate commerce regulation in the United States.

In the popular view, SP, the Big Guys, relying on land use decisions by Congress and the courts, used the might of their wealth to get the support they needed for railroad routes in California while oppressing the little man, a jerk thing to do. The Mussel Slough shootists, the Little Guys, despite gaining immediate hero status, would have been jerks and worse if they truly did shoot without provocation. The truth will always be a little murky, but multiple "jerk-ness" was rampant in May 1880 at Mussel Slough.

WAR IN TULARE
EJECTMENT PROCESS RESISTED
BLOODY WORK OVER DISPUTED TITLES

San Francisco, May 11—Contest between the railroad company and settlers on lands claimed by the company in what is known as Mussel Slough District, in Tulare and Fresno Counties, culminated today in a tragedy. United States Marshal Poole left here a day or two ago to serve writs of ejectment on certain settlers, by virtue of decision of the Circuit Court, in favor of the railroad company. This afternoon Deputy Marshal Worth, of this city, received the following dispatch from Marshal Poole: "In attempting to execute the writ four men were killed and two wounded." No further particulars are yet received. The settlers are banded together for mutual protection, and express a determination to resist all attempts at ejectment.
—SACRAMENTO DAILY RECORD-UNION, MAY 13, 1880

David versus Goliath played well in the sensational May 1880 news story: Noble settlers' land rights in colorfully named Mussel Slough were being snatched away for profit by fat cat California railroad industrialists. The *real* story—whatever version—revealed jerks in each camp.

Did a nervous horse kick US Marshal Alonzo W. Poole down, as he recalled for the railroad company, causing everyone to panic and grab guns? Or, perhaps someone shouted out, guns were drawn, tempers flared, and shots were fired? No one present at squatter

Henry Brewer's Mussel Slough residence on May 11, 1880, later remembered exactly the same cascade of bloody events or who or what started the gunfight. But, when the federal marshal's' attempt to evict squatters was over, seven men were dead and five men later judged guilty were about to become celebrated local heroes.

The *Sacramento Daily Record-Union* newspaper reporter raced to the scene:

> *The report of this awful occurrence, which occurred about 10 o'clock, spread like wildfire. It reached Hanford in about an hour, and a reporter instantly started for the scene of action, and was soon on the ground. A sickening spectacle met his gaze. Stretched on the porch of Brewer's house were the bloody and lifeless remains of James M. Harris, Iver Knutson and John E. Henderson, while the fourth form was that of D. M. Hartt, writhing and groaning from a mortal wound in the abdomen.*

Readers could drink up the details:

> *Inside the house was a no less ghastly spectacle. On one bed was Dan Kelly, terribly wounded, with three holes in his back, and on another couch Arch McGregor lay groaning with three horrid wounds through his body.*

Walter Crow, wounded, ran from the Brewer place and died later.

Most of the community had been at a Hanford picnic that doubled as a meeting to rally local support for those protesting the railroad's land use. The speaker was supposed to be the volatile David S. Terry, who did not appear, but he sent his speech to be read instead.

At Mussel Slough:

> *The wives, children and friends soon began to arrive, and their piercing shrieks and heartrending cries filled the air.*

What had sparked the Battle at Mussel Slough?

With both the 1849–1850s Gold Rush and the 1860s Comstock Lode silver mine boom in Nevada played out, slower westward expansion into California continued via grueling desert and mountain overland routes or by a months-long sea voyage around Cape Horn. Prospective California settlers included former Confederate army soldiers and officers looking for new land and opportunities. Most new arrivals ended up in the cities, especially in San Francisco, the state's economic and social hub, though some sought their own land in the hinterlands.

On May 10, 1869, the Transcontinental Railroad, built from the east by the Union Pacific Railroad and westward by the Central Pacific Railroad, met at Promontory Summit, Utah. When Central Pacific president Leland Stanford swung to drive the last, solid gold spike into the track, flesh-and-blood horses, like those of the legendary 1860 Pony Express Riders, were instantly replaced on the east-west route by the "Iron Horse." Steam locomotive–pulled trains that moved people and freight to either side of the country without the need to stop for rest, horse and rider provisions, geography, or weather delays.

Settlers in California's San Joaquin Valley, the Central Valley, who trickled in were beginning to irrigate and cultivate its fertile but dry soil. The generally arid valley had mighty rivers flowing from mountains to the east, the Sierra Nevada, onto its plain and into occasional marshes and tributaries. One tributary of the Kings River (named for the Biblical Three Kings) created Mussel Slough. By 1880, there was a Mussel Slough District between Hanford and Lemoore, railroad towns that had been built a few years before to service the anticipated Southern Pacific Railroad route between San Jose and Southern California.

The Southern Pacific story began three decades before the shoot-out at Mussel Slough, when California's isolating geography begged to be conquered by steam locomotives. Speculators, entrepreneurs, and engineers such as Theodore D. Judah were determined to at least connect California's cities and major towns by rail. The Holy Grail for Judah and the others, including Washington politicians, was an all-weather train route across the Sierra Nevada and beyond to the Midwest and eastern seaboard markets—a transcontinental railway.

In 1860, while Judah worked for another railroad designing a route from Sacramento, over the Sierra, and on to the Comstock Lode silver mines near Virginia City, Nevada, he determined that Donner Pass (where the Donner Party had been caught in record winter snows thirteen years before) would be the best mountain crossing. Though called crazy when he insisted on the deep snow route, Judah finally persuaded backers to set up the Central Pacific Railroad Company (CP). The original CP investors lacked incorporation money. Judah promoted his own company and route relentlessly to Sacramento business people and others.

By spring 1861, the engineer had the support of Sacramento hardware store partners Collis P. Huntington and Mark Hopkins, as well as Sacramento merchants Leland Stanford and Charles Crocker. Their funds backed June 1861 Central Pacific Railroad incorporation, ensuring a rail line that Judah and the others hoped just might extend beyond Nevada to connect with the long-proposed eastern transcontinental railroad route.

Associates Huntington, Hopkins, Stanford, and Crocker, the "Big Four," as they became known, had supported the anti-slavery Republican Party whose 1860 elected candidate was President Abraham Lincoln. Stanford was elected California's governor in 1861. CP's Huntington and engineer Judah travelled to Washington, DC, to lobby Congress, where Judah served as railway committee clerk to both Congressional houses' committees. CP stock, then worth only the value of its paper, was given to anyone who could or would support the CP route.

The Pacific Railway Act of 1862, passed despite the raging Civil War, authorized the Union Pacific and Central Pacific Railroads to begin construction of the Transcontinental Railroad, a route through the center of the United States. This "northern" transcontinental route was completed in 1869. Because of known terrain and weather challenges along the Union Pacific–CP route, a similar southern route was considered. The Southern Pacific Railroad, founded in 1865, hoped to build the southern line terminus from San Jose to the Colorado River at the California-Arizona Territory border. The Big Four bought the SP, its proposed route, and rights in 1868. An SP line was to extend down the Central Valley into the region near Mussel Slough.

Allocation of land was crucial in westward migration and settlement. In 1862, the same year the original Pacific Railroad Act became law, the Homestead Act also laid out land claim provisions.

The issue and quarrel at Mussel Slough was over the rights to settle on, improve, assert squatters' rights to, or buy at a cheap price the odd-numbered sections of the checkerboard land description laid out in the Railway Acts. Rights and ownership of land grants should have been clear. They were not.

SEC. 3. And be it further enacted, That there be, and is hereby, granted to the said company, for the purpose of aiding in the construction of said railroad and telegraph line, and to secure the safe and speedy, transportation of the mails, troops, munitions of war, and public stores thereon, every alternate section of public land, designated by odd numbers, to the amount of five [Sec. 4, Act of 1864 changed the amount to ten] *alternate sections per mile on each side of said railroad, on the line thereof, and within the limits of ten miles* [Sec. 4, Act of 1864 changed the grant to twenty miles] *on each side of said road, not sold, reserved, or otherwise disposed of by the United States, and to which a preemption or homestead claim may not have attached, at the time the line of said road is definitely fixed: provided, That all mineral lands shall be excepted from the operation of this act; but where the same shall contain timber, the timber thereon is hereby granted to said company. And all such lands so granted by this section which shall not be sold or disposed of by*

*said company within three years after the entire road
shall have been completed, shall be subject to settlement
and pre-emption like other lands, at a price not exceeding
one dollar and twenty-five cents per acre, to be paid to
said company.*
—Pacific Railroad Act, July 1, 1862 (with 1864 Act changes)

Secretaries of the interior had muddied the waters by backing and forthing on whether the odd-numbered sections of public land belonged wholly to the railroad, or whether the line would have to be built first as the law required before the land was sold. Once the line was built, the federal government could issue land-grant patents that gave a legal document with title to the land to the railroad. Legally, the land remained in the public domain until that moment. Special terms for railroad companies, like issuance of bonds by the US government to fund construction and granting of timber and other resource rights to help the building, helped the CP, Union Pacific, and eventually, the SP to get the nationally mandated rail system built.

Beginning in 1876, the CP and SP had widely distributed posters targeted at transporting laborers and emigrants to land the companies had for sale in California, Nevada, and Utah. C. P. Huntington undersigned the poster's Southern Pacific Railroad language authorizing an SP offer of "a vast extent of land," a grant that included some of the best coastal, valley, and wheat-producing land. Orchards, wine, cotton, tobacco, and cattle raising were also touted.

The fine point of whether the railroad, SP, had built the rail line out and had sections certified as properly American-built and safe to receive the government land patents was not always clear in the marketing or actions of the railroad officials.

Some arrivals headed for land to settle on and built houses. Some started irrigation projects with other indications of permanent settlement. Some had been there before the railroad arrived and their rights to hold and keep the land were protected. And, there were the public even-numbered sections next to the odd-numbered tracts involved with railroad rights.

At Mussel Slough, the issue quickly became legal residence versus squatting, taking over the land just by being on it. Some settlers insisted that SP was offering to sell the land to them for more than the legally authorized price—$17 or $40 an acre instead of $2.50 per acre—when the settlers themselves had paid for improvements. With all these bristly issues swirling around and neighbors vying for shares of available land in 1877, the SP had finished enough of the Mussel Slough District line to qualify for government land patents.

Settlers who filed homestead claims and squatters began to flow into the Mussel Slough area in the early 1870s. The lure of free or almost-free land offered by SP was strong, and it led to some land speculation-buying and selling of land that SP might sell to them some day at a very cheap price.

Indiana-born John J. Doyle sold his original California farm in 1870 and moved near Mussel Slough where he, along with other squatters, intended to challenge the SP's Central Valley route. As anger roiled, Doyle and Major Thomas Jefferson McQuiddy organized the Settlers' Grand League in 1878. Many members of this armed private militia were Confederate war veterans. Doyle urged local residents to file land claims with the local land office in Visalia while using the league's resources to file suits against SP. The league had brought Dennis Kearney of the Workingmen's Party to speak to those living around the Mussel Slough area in spring 1880.

Whether league leaders fomented the restlessness that led to the May 11 shootings, deadly jerk behavior, or not, Major McQuiddy addressed a turnout in Hanford on May 14. As reported in the *Sacramento Daily Record-Union,* he publically denied the league's involvement and placed blame elsewhere.

The Settler's League, as an organization, has endeavored to keep the peace and live under the law of this land. Many things have been done upon the part of those not in sympathy with us to arouse you to action, to prompt you to do that which was not in keeping with good citizenship. Some of you are neighbors who have not seen proper to join in this legal fight with the league, who sympathize with you in your struggle, but have been charged with being your enemies. I say, in many instances, that is untrue. They have been misrepresented to a very great extent. Only a few days ago notices were going the rounds, being delivered through the mail, to certain parties to leave the county, and signed as being by order of the league.

I said then upon the start to parties who received such notices that they were without authority; that the league was doing no such business. It was done, fellow-citizens, to work up a disturbance. How much it did to add to the tragedy of the week is not for me to say; yet I am satisfied that it did something in that direction.

Southern Pacific officials maintained that they were pure and legal in their dealings and entitled to sell the land as they chose at prices the railroad set. A corporate attorney cited a decision issued by a federal court in 1879 that affirmed SP's right to sell land.

The dispute raged in the press: At San Francisco's sandlot meeting place, Workingmen's Party supporters adopted resolutions of support for the Mussel Slough protesters, as quoted in the *Sacramento Daily Record-Union* on May 17.

As fellow stragglers against the rapacious and overshadowing greed of corporate juggernauts, to send cheer to those unfortunate, yet noble, people of Tulare county, who in defense of their homes, firesides, children and principles, are making such heroic resistance, and amidst the most flagrant and treacherous disregard of solemn obligations by their oppressors have already yielded five valuable lives.

The resolutions go on to mention:

Bones of the land robbers and railroad thieves will be left to bleach on the plains. Resolved, That we will warn these settlers of the duplicity and treachery of the corporation with whom they are dealing.

What happened at Mussel Slough depends on who told the story.

Mills Hartt and Walter Crow had recently purchased SP railroad land, already occupied by some of the Mussel Slough squatters. Acting with a writ from a federal judge, US Marshal Poole, SP land-grader William Clark, Hartt, and Crow set off early in the morning for Grangeville, near Hanford. Henry Brewer's homestead was first. Twenty, forty, or fifty men with weapons blocked the way and demanded that the marshal, Clark, and the others surrender their guns. Poole and Clark refused. Later in the day, Poole reported back to Deputy US Marshal Worth in San Francisco that a horse had kicked him at that moment.

Shouting started, guns were fired, and in the end, five settler-squatters were dead, as were land buyers Hartt, and Crow who died shortly after. Unscathed, Poole and Clark had not fired.

No one was tried for murder. Public sentiment quickly backed the settlers and those who had stood up to SP's land-sale enforcement, although not everyone believed Major McQuiddy's claim that the league had not been involved in the Mussel Slough incident. By the end of the year, a small group of men, including Doyle, were on trial in San Francisco to presumably remove the trial from feelings running high in Tulare County.

Attending the trial, a *San Francisco Examiner* reporter observed, "They look like quiet, respectable-looking farmers."

Two days before Christmas, five of the accused, including Doyle, were convicted of interfering with and obstructing a US marshal while he was lawfully executing a writ of a United States Court, though not of conspiracy to resist the federal official, a charge with much more severe penalties. The sentence was eight months' incarceration, a $300 fine, and costs.

It was Marshal Poole who escorted the men to serve time in the Santa Clara County Jail, in San Jose. Prison facilities were large and described as humane and comfortable. James M. Patterson's family moved in with him. The jailer left the door unlocked. Fund-raising events were held to raise money for the prisoners' food and to support their families. A chef-inmate cooked for the men.

The local papers published comments by the prisoners. Some of the prisoners attended church or lodge meetings outside the jail. Visitors came by constantly. Mail, letters of support, were posted from all over the world. And, not long after the oyster dinner to celebrate the end of the prison terms on September 23, 1881, ex-prisoner William Baden, now well-known as one of the Mussel Slough heroes, married the jailer's daughter at a local fine hotel. Doyle returned to Lemoore and became justice of the peace.

In the end, although some families left the area, many Mussel Slough residents, including Doyle, paid a reduced price for railroad land in a compromise suggested by one of the Big Four, Charles Crocker.

Resentments against the perceived railroad company monopolies whose rights were enforced in federal courts had come to violence in the incoherent Mussel Slough shooting deaths. Legal arguments aside, similar, if not violent disputes between railroads and settlers were boiling over elsewhere. The public clamored for protection against the Big Guys, the monopolies that appeared to hold all the cards, financial and legal.

In January 1881, a month after the incarceration of the Mussel Slough Five, the Anti-Monopoly League met at New York's Cooper Institute to oppose "gigantic" railroad and telegraph wire monopolies. Local chapters were organized, including one in Hanford.

The railroads were under scrutiny.

In 1887, six years after the Mussel Slough Five served their time for obstruction of a federal official, the US Congress passed the Interstate Commerce Act, making it unlawful and discriminatory for any transportation provider, including a railroad, to give more favorable terms to any customers or other companies.

Yet the bad taste lingered with resentment of the Southern Pacific monopoly that lasted well into the next century.

SOURCES

Polarized views of what happened at Mussel Slough developed immediately. The concept of a big corporation throwing its weight around and wronged little guy settlers was fodder for muckrakers, novelists, poets, and interviewers for decades. Frank Norris's 1901 novel, *The Octopus: A Story of California* (New York: Doubleday, Page & Co.), was taken for gospel truth, although Norris changed incidents and details in his fictionalized account.

Terry Beers introduces and edits selections from Norris, poet Ambrose Bierce, and others in *Gunfight at Mussel Slough: Evolution of a Western Myth* (Berkeley, Calif.: Heyday Books, 2004). A vast, empty, dry valley in the West to be converted to agriculture was a theme in Americans' migration west. The westward push was helped by railroads expanding their tracks and routes but hindered by rail regulations and government policy that restricted or controlled the land.

J. L. Brown, in his 1958 book, *The Mussel Slough Tragedy* (Third Printing, Lemoore, Calif.: Kings River Press, 2001), narrates the showdown and shoot-out story seen from a perspective almost eighty years after the incident. Brown undertook a thorough review of contemporary newspapers, trial court proceedings, and childhood memories of some of the settler-participants. Brown used newspaper accounts and trial testimony to personally walk the Mussel Slough Battle site and map the setting. In pinpointing the known details, his aim was to dispel ambitious people using one side in the controversy to prove a point of view: SP as evil, for example, and the other side as virtuous.

Richard J. Orsi, professor emeritus of history at California State University, East Bay, was offered total access to archival Southern Pacific Railroad records, and in 2005, the University of

California Press, Berkeley, California, published his lengthy, modern appreciation of railroad involvement in California's growth and development, *Sunset Unlimited: The Southern Pacific Railroad and the Development of the American West 1850–1930,* which describes the laws and tactics that affected central California land settlement policies and railroad dealings.

The virtual Central Pacific Railroad Photographic History Museum, http://CPRR.org, is a comprehensive, privately maintained website about the building of the Transcontinental Railroad with text of or links to documents, press reports, and many images including photographs, tickets, and posters.

The Pacific Railway Act (1862), Homestead Act (1862), and the Interstate Commerce Act (1887) are among 100 Milestone Documents from the US National Archives and Records Administration shown with summaries and full text at http://ourdocuments.gov.

CHAPTER 10

Chinatown Gangster
Big Trouble for "Little Pete"

One jerk from the 'hood lived a life of crime and was taken out by hit men when his guard was lowered just a little. It's a tale ripped from modern headlines: A hardened inner-city gangster got what he deserved and died young.

The story of Fong Jing Toy could be unfolding in many of today's inner city neighborhoods, but his 'hood was San Francisco's Chinatown more than a century ago. While many of Chinatown's inhabitants were hard-working and law-abiding, he was not. Power, control, and wealth were his. To one and all in the white world, including a special police force vice squad that watched Chinatown, he was known and feared as "Little Pete."

Little Pete was luxuriating in a free moment in a Chinatown barber's chair, ready to order a favorite German #4 sandwich from the delicatessen. Unbeknownst to him, these breaths in anticipation of a splendid hair treatment, clean-shaven forehead, ear cleaning, and delicious meal were to be his last. He was settling down to have his long, well-kept pigtail, the symbol of his heritage from imperial China, unbraided and cared for by the barber. After all, late January 1897 was a time of celebration in San Francisco's Chinatown, when the Lunar New Year was about to change from the Year of the Monkey to that of the lucky Rooster.

All Chinatown felt festive, cleaned, and decorated in red and gold for the New Year. Little Pete was king of it all, the King of Chinatown, feared by all who lived there, especially those criminals in the community's underbelly who had crossed him. At the same time, all of Chinatown felt tension surge when the celebratory firecrackers that were traditionally set off at the New Year to chase

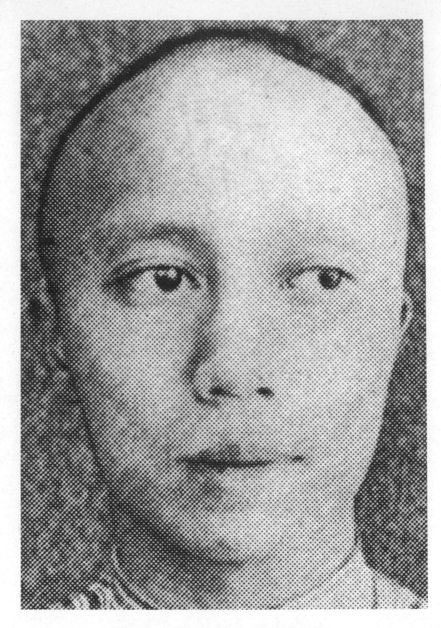

Fong Jing Toy, also known as Little Pete
COURTESY SAN FRANCISCO HISTORY CENTER, SAN FRANCISCO PUBLIC LIBRARY

away demons exploded randomly with a *pop-pop-pop-pop-pop* that sounded like gunfire. It made everyone hoping for a peaceful and prosperous New Year just a little more anxious that tong violence was about to escalate.

Little Pete was head of the Sum Yop Tong, and had been its leader for almost a decade. His real name was either Fong Jing or Fong Ching Toy. Little Pete was in his early thirties. He was the brain that directed the tong's operation. He had the business acumen to guide the mostly illegal businesses that let him take his share of the profits from prostitution, opium dens, gambling, and a thriving slave trade in women and girls. Among the twenty or so Chinatown tongs, the Sum Yop members were exceptionally prosperous, in part from the legitimate businesses and factories that were their fronts to cover even more lucrative illegal operations.

Tongs developed during the California Gold Rush when Chinese miners were discriminated against, harassed, and driven out of the mines. California's tongs began as mutual aid and protection groups, but sometimes warfare erupted between competing tongs. As Chinese men eventually gravitated toward the major city, *Dabu,* or "First City" (San Francisco) and its Chinatown, so did the tongs.

There, the tongs battled viciously for power, acting very much like the modern feuding crime families associated with organized crime. There were godfather-like chieftains and their enforcers, "soldiers" called *boo how doy*. They obeyed the tong leader's orders unquestioningly, whether it was to extort payments or carry out an assassination. *Boo how doy* soldiers were the tong hit men, distinctive with their pigtail queues wound up around their heads, fixed under a dark slouch hat that offered some anonymity. The white world called these hatchetmen "highbinders." Unlike the usual flowing tunic top worn by Chinese men, the highbinders wore shirts tied with belts that carried the weapon of choice—a knife, hatchet, stick, or gun—usually left with the victim's body at the crime scene. *Boo how doy* were given hazardous duty benefits, including a $500 death payment, medical care, paid medical leave, a disability payment with a return trip to China, and compensation for each year of jail time served.

San Francisco Chinatown's tong wars began in 1875. Rivalries were sparked by insults or competitions for underworld profits. Little Pete may have watched the first pitched battle between the Suey Sing Tong and the Kwong Duck Tong from the balcony or window of a building at Washington Street, above Waverly Place. No record exists of Fong Jing's date of birth in Canton, China, in the 1860s, but he was about ten years old when he saw the first hatchet, knife, and club battle between *boo how doy* from rival tongs shedding blood in the small street below. He had been in the United States for five years, a merchant's clever son sent to school—or at least Sunday School—at the Chinese Methodist Mission. Unlike many Chinese, Little Pete spoke perfect English.

Little Pete operated in Chinatown's streets before the 1906 Earthquake and Fire reduced the enclave to ruins. In the late nineteenth century, his Chinatown was a lively world, largely unknown to white outsiders except for its vices: opium dens and Chinese prostitutes, which horrified and titillated Victorians. Horse-drawn carriages and wooden delivery wagons rolled down cobble-lined streets. Tom Yun Gai (Sacramento Street) where the earliest settlers had built homes above storefronts had given way to its parallel street, Dupont Gai (Grant Avenue), one block east. Portsmouth Square was still the meeting place it had been since the American flag was raised there fifty years before.

Little Pete, an obvious target for rival tongs' *boo how doy,* took care not to be taken. There was talk of a murderous dog guarding the door of his windowless bedroom. Whenever he emerged, several white bodyguards, supposedly immune to attack by tong members, flanked him. His own *boo how doy* were nearby to protect their leader who wore chain mail body armor and sported a metal-lined hat.

When Little Pete did go outside, he entered a twelve-square-block world inhabited by twenty-thousand men. Women, except for occasional female servants and for one special holiday each year, did not leave their homes, or houses of prostitution. The buildings densely packed with residents were several stories high, with wooden balconies and occasional awnings. Huge red paper lanterns, birdcages, or laundry hung from some balconies. Sidewalk street vendors served steamed food from woven baskets or mats, cobblers mended shoes, and men who told fortunes were mostly hired to write letters, many enclosing money, back to families in China. There were temples, a few Christian churches and missions, and opium dens in the back rooms of stores. Bazaars, the equivalent of general stores, sold groceries, tea, lacquered wooden objects, silk, small porcelain pots, kites, and the then-legal opium. Other stores sold dry goods and bedding, folded and neatly arranged in floor-to-second-story glass cases. If a man felt unwell, a Chinese herbalist would feel his pulse, then pull out small quantities of herbs, roots, and dried flowers from hundreds of boxes and porcelain jars around the walls of the Chinese pharmacy to mix them to treat the diagnosed illness. There were butchers with meat hanging in view, preserved meat shops with duck carcasses displayed on hooks, fishmongers with local shrimp and squid, and live chickens sold door-to-door from baskets by men carrying poles across their shoulders. It smelled of meat, steaming rice, noodle broth, baked savory buns, sweet incense, and sewage.

Little Pete could walk the streets and know where his profits came from: the rackets operating behind closed doors. Some streets and alleys were specialized by type of business. The infamous Street of the Gamblers catered to lotteries and games of fan tan, all well hidden with multiple doors and watchers to signal the approach of police. Little Pete got his cut from the profits. The opium rooms catered to Chinese and whites, offering the legal drug of reclining forgetfulness inhaled through a long pipe. Platforms of wood topped by wooden mats and head pillows were the basic furnishings, with hooks on the walls for jackets and hats. Little Pete got his cut from the opium resorts, as they were known, too. His operatives could enforce the protection racket, where merchants paid to insure that the tong would not damage the storefront or inventory. Little Pete had some of that action.

He could pass the street-level doors with grills over their single windows where Chinese, and occasionally even white female eyes stared at him, the tong boss. The prostitutes, two to six to a tiny twelve-foot-by-fourteen-foot space, were confined to this "crib" and engaged in sexual acts with whomever they could attract through the window by wheedling and listing prices for services. Some were slaves, abandoned on the street, kidnapped, or given up by their families in China to someone who arranged to have the girl, age two or older, transported and sold in a Chinatown basement auction. Some auctioned women were bought as real wives for Chinese men who in the 1890 US Census outnumbered Chinese women twenty-seven to one, and lived in a bachelor society. Other females were bought as house servants, but most ended up as sex slaves. Another arrangement was a contract that required that the girl or woman repay the costs of her passage to California and expenses to maintain her to the man who bought her contract. If she was confined as a prostitute, her standard contract added time if she took sick time, and if she ran away, she was to be a slave for life.

No matter how degraded the individual women were, to Little Pete, they were part of another racket, made more valuable when the US Congress passed the Chinese Exclusion Act in 1882. Since then, Little Pete knew, few Chinese women had arrived in the United States, hidden in a cargo hold, via Canada, or being claimed as a wife by someone who would often sell her instead. After 1882, scarce women had become an even more valuable commodity, especially if they could make a profit for someone. The prostitution racket even benefited from young white men who wanted to have a peep, a ten cent "lookee," at the Chinese woman's genitalia, widely rumored to be anatomically different from those with European ancestry. It all added up, and Little Pete got his cut from prostitution, too.

San Francisco's Police Department had always been challenged by the crime and frequent enough violence in Chinatown streets. The tongs were the bane of the officers' existence, but often enough, the source of income or other favors. No one knows when the "Chinatown Squad" officially got its mandate, but by the 1880s, it was functioning as a vice squad, overseeing Chinatown, closing illegal operations, and trying to control the tong warfare. Eventually, to prevent graft, the department declared that all officers would have short assignments in the squad. It didn't work. Certain officers who could work with the Chinese, or were favored by the Chinese Six Companies benevolent association, the tongs, or merchants might have several tours of duty. They wore plain clothes, and, as whites, they were obvious, yet not in any official uniform. The Chinatown Squad was equipped with long knives, guns, axes, or sledgehammers.

Today, the San Francisco Sheriff's Department website posts Little Pete's mug shot as one of its "Infamous Inmates." On July 28, 1886, one of Little Pete's bodyguards, Lee Chuck, shot a rival tong member to death. San Francisco policeman John Martin of the Chinatown Squad pursued Lee Chuck, who missed when he fired at Martin. Lee Chuck was arrested.

Before Lee Chuck's trial, Little Pete offered Martin money to not testify. It was attempted bribery, and Martin wasted no time in arresting Little Pete. Little Pete was tried three times amid jury tampering. Little Pete maintained that he had offered the bribe as a bribe, but that he refused to pay more when Martin and others returned to demand additional bribes. A jury finally convicted him on the third go-around.

Sentenced to five years in San Quentin State Prison for attempted bribery, Little Pete served eighteen months. As he left prison, he told reporters that he was going to go into business. The legitimate business he set up was F. C. Peters & Company, a shoe factory with Chinese workers.

But, Little Pete was anything but finished with tongs and tong lifestyle.

In 1888, the year Little Pete emerged from San Quentin, Patrolman Bill Price was assigned to the Chinatown Squad. By

1890, he was a sergeant and head of the Chinatown Ssquad. His methodology was to take action, even if it violated the letter of the law and constitutional rights. He approached his police chief, Patrick Crowley, asking for permission to break up the tongs, their headquarters, and to scatter tong members. After he was refused, Price enlisted the support of the Chinese Consul General whose office usually protected its citizens but was tired of the vicious tong wars. It agreed to refuse to protect tong members and to indemnify the chief of police from any suits by Chinese. In 1891, Chief Crowley authorized Price's Chinatown Squad raids on the tongs. Furnishings were smashed, the offices and meeting rooms rendered useless, weapons were seized, and no one was allowed to re-enter. Squadmen then approached the merchants and operators of the houses of prostitution and told them that extortion they had experienced wouldn't be tolerated any longer.

The tongs were not down for long. In 1896, the Chinese Consul again agreed that Sergeant Price's men could conduct more anti-tong raids. More headquarters were raided, furniture smashed to splinters, and any operatives found inside were kicked down the stairs.

But some on the Chinatown Squad were on the take from gambling "resorts" and others who paid the police to leave them and their operations alone. Decades before, the San Francisco Police Department had decreed that Chinatown Squad members would be rotated out after serving six months. That policy wasn't always followed, so a policeman could be taking bribes, if he had the cooperation of or similar collusion with those about him, wherever he was assigned in the city. Chinatown's profitable underworld enterprises and the tongs were happy to make that happen when officers and patrolmen were willing. In 1894, the police chief was shown evidence of Chinatown Squad corruption and hired private detectives to verify the details. For years, the police clerk had been assigning Chinatown Squad member rotation and alerting the squad head whenever a raid on Chinatown was about to go down. Greater Chinatown was warned in advance. The 1894 scandal when many policemen were suddenly fired without explanation had blown up publicly and made speculative newspaper headlines.

Little Pete, along with other leaders in the world of vice, contributed to a police bribery fund. In 1896, his interest in gambling extended to his own sizeable bets placed on horses at Bay District and Ingleside race tracks. Long shots won so consistently that Little Pete was reported to have raked in one hundred thousand dollars from betting on winners. Track officials were suspicious and hired private detectives who discovered that some jockeys were getting bribes from Little Pete to throw races or to poison specific horses. Those jockeys and Little Pete were banned from the tracks for life, but Little Pete had made a fortune.

The other tongs hated Little Pete and his Sum Yop operatives. Little Pete had even integrated his tong as the Sum Yop Company into the umbrella Chinatown benevolent association group organization, the Chinese Six Companies. As a high official, Little Pete was one of the men who represented Chinatown and its interests to the world.

Organized crime could not afford one all-controlling tong or its leader. The movement to end Little Pete's dominance was led by his arch rivals in the Sue Yop Tong. In 1896, the Sue Yops convened a meeting with twelve other tongs and issued a four-part death warrant against Little Pete. It accused him of preventing merchants from bringing their wives into the United States; that he had paid one thousand dollars in gold to have a fellow Chinese killed by *boo how doy;* ordered Lee Chuck to kill the innocent head hatchetman of a rival tong; and had prevented the tongs' peace agreement.

Word spread that the tongs had authorized a reward of three thousand dollars for the death of Little Pete. Tong leaders assigned men to keep track of Little Pete's movements at all times. The reward came with tong assurance to any assassin that he would be protected against charges of murder and a trial. The tongs would ensure his disappearance after the deed was done.

Little Pete was well aware of the bounty staked for his life and slept with the dog outside his door, no windows in his sleeping quarters, and was never without his bodyguards.

Well, almost never. Perhaps he felt that the New Year celebrations would distract attention away from him. Or perhaps his need for a New Year barber visit with a favorite sandwich was too tempting. For whatever reason, Little Pete descended from his third-floor room at 819 Washington Street by an interior staircase to the bottom floor barber shop with only one bodyguard in attendance. For a few minutes, Little Pete relaxed his guard and sent the bodyguard out to purchase a newspaper. It was a fatal mistake.

The fatal moment was pieced together afterward, embellished and shifted in the details over time. What is known and surmised was that two Chinese men from Oregon had heard about the reward, traveled to San Francisco, and had been waiting for their opportunity while stalking their mark. They entered the barber shop as if they were clients and waited until the barber was about to begin with Little Pete, whose neck above his body armor would be vulnerable to any approach. Lee Jung moved quickly to Little Pete's neck and fired a .45 caliber revolver downward to breach the vital organs. The other assassin, Chew Chin Gop, also fired into Little Pete's head before both men fled to a building across Waverly Place.

No police on duty had been watching Little Pete's movements. When officers arrived shortly after the shots resounded down the street, they found him dead, and the barber murmured something about not seeing anything. In the street outside were a revolver and a shotgun. Hearing that the perpetrators had fled into a Waverly Place building, the police raced in and arrested the four men they found, including two well-known tong hatchetmen wearing their weapons who were playing cards.

San Francisco was horrified at the bloody murder, but relieved that the notorious Little Pete was dead. What about his tong and its inevitable revenge? A bloodbath began and then stopped when the Chinese Emperor's representative imprisoned all the relatives of Little Pete's opposing tongs who still lived in China until the violence ended.

The two Oregon hit men got away. The card-playing hatch-etmen were tried for murder but acquitted. The San Francisco police entered Chinatown en masse three days after Little Pete's assassination and spent two days searching the tongs' headquarters, smashing the contents, and arresting anyone considered a "highbinder." Two weeks later, they again entered and searched highbinder homes and businesses. For a few years, the tong wars in San Francisco's Chinatown went dormant.

For Little Pete, a.k.a. Fong Jing/Ching Toy, all that remained was a proper funeral. His body was gowned magnificently, lest anyone sending him to heaven risk revenge from his spirit. There was a regal black hearse carriage, bands, priests, an official cortege of more than one hundred carriages through Chinatown, and wagons full of food and beverages, including tea and gin, for Little Pete's final "banquet" before burial at the cemetery. At the gravesite altar, the meal was spread out amid incense and chanting by the priests. But the crowd couldn't wait any longer and lunged for the food and drink, turning a solemn occasion into a riot. Even in death, Little Pete managed to disturb the peace.

SOURCES

Kevin J. Mullen, retired San Francisco deputy police chief, wrote *Chinatown Squad* (Novato, Calif.: Noir Publications, 2008) that covers Chinese criminal activities in San Francisco's Chinatown from Gold Rush times to the current century. The police department's Chinatown Squad and Gang Task Force were at various times responsible for "Policing the Dragon," including the activities of Little Pete. Mullen also includes a chapter on Little Pete in his 2005 book, *The Toughest Gang in Town: Police Stories from Old San Francisco* (Novato, Calif.: Noir Publications, 2005). Charles F. Adams's "Revenge of the Tongs—1897" chapter describes the career of Little Pete in *Murder by the Bay: Historic Homicide in and about the City of San Francisco* (Sanger, Calif.: Word Dancer Press, 2005).

Ivan Light, professor of sociology at the University of California, Los Angeles deftly wrote the article, "From Vice District to Tourist Attraction: The Moral Career of American Chinatowns, 1880–1940" for the *Pacific Historical Review* (Vol. 43, No. 3, August 1974), describing how filthy and sordid American Chinatowns were before the image of them as being quaint places to have Chinese food became the dominant impression for non-Chinese.

The late journalist and editor Herbert Asbury wrote *The Barbary Coast: An Informal History of the San Francisco Underground* classic in 1933 (New York: reprint Basic Books, 2002). His chapter, "The Slaves of Chinatown" has a riveting description of Little Pete, his activities, the tongs, prostitution, and other Chinatown vice.

The treatment of Chinese women is passionately described in "The Woman's Tale" chapter of *Driven Out: The Forgotten War against Chinese Americans* (New York: Random House, 2007), by University of Maryland professor of English, East Asian Studies, and Women's Studies, Jean Pfaelzer.

Two photographic books show San Francisco's Chinatown's streets, shops, and people before the 1906 Earthquake and Fire destroyed its buildings. Judy Yung and the Chinese Historical Society of America gathered the images in *San Francisco's Chinatown* (Charleston, So. Carolina: Arcadia Publishing, 2006). *Historic Photos of the Chinese in California,* by Hannah Clayborn (Nashville, Tenn.: Turner Publishing Company, 2009), includes a chapter on San Francisco's "Old Chinatown." Two short films by Thomas Edison, Inc. in the Library of Congress Motion Picture, Broadcasting and Recorded Sound Division bring Chinatown in Little Pete's era to life: *Arrest in Chinatown* (http://hdl.loc.gov/loc.mbrsmi/lcmp003.m3a15145, circa 1897) and *San Francisco Chinese Funeral* (procession through Chinatown for Tom Kim Yung, http://hdl.loc.gov/loc.mbrsmi/lcmp003.m3a12311, 1903).

CHAPTER 11

Corruption at City Hall
San Francisco's Boss Abe Ruef
Gets the Rap

At the dawn of the twentieth century, the city was a cesspit of corruption. Graft was a fact of life in San Francisco. Many politicians could be bribed. Contractors, labor unions, small businessmen, capitalists, and government employees were buying into making easy money with their payoffs. Pay something to get something. They were jerks for ripping off investors and the citizenry.

The man who could arrange it all and skim from the take was San Francisco's political fixer, Abe Ruef. They called him the Curly Boss, the Kingmaker. He made his man the mayor of San Francisco.

Then the earth trembled and jolted in the early morning of April 18, 1906. Investigations into corruption that were already under way gained momentum after the Great Earthquake and Fire. Ruef and his mayor stood trial. Ruef, the jerk who had "fixed" the city, became the fall guy for a jerk-filled era.

In 1908, Abe Ruef was forty-four years old. He was one of the most despised politicians in America. Yet, he never held elective office.

It took five ballots for the jury to render a guilty verdict on December 10, 1908. For the single bribery conviction, San Francisco's most notorious political boss was sentenced to spend fourteen years in San Quentin Prison. His enemies gloated. One-time allies saved their own reputations at his expense. He was going to prison, but the others involved were not. Promised immunity from prosecution had been withdrawn. It wasn't justice. It wasn't fair. They had played with him. This was not how it was supposed to be. . .

Abe Ruef
COURTESY SAN FRANCISCO HISTORY CENTER, SAN FRANCISCO PUBLIC LIBRARY

Folks had thought that San Francisco had learned its lesson. The Gold Rush population boom of 1849 had brought with it all the problems of an instant society: criminals, murderers, pickpockets, prostitutes, petty thieves, gamblers, robbers, and ne'er-do-wells, all trying to make a killing or at least a living by shuffling around in the background of society, despised and suspect. Jerks all.

Half a century later, not much had changed. The crimes and sins of the Barbary Coast were catalogued in newspapers, sensational and lurid recitals of murders and robberies and fallen women. Periodic cleanups swept the brothels, gambling houses, and Chinatown's houses of ill repute, gambling parlors, and opium dens. The cleanups were usually temporary. Money changed hands to protect the illicit enterprises. The houses, parlors, and dens quickly reopened.

Political and economic influence was peddled. Occasional reformers spoke out, and periodically there were attempts to sweep clean the police department, city government, and the office appointments that were normally the prerogative of the politically powerful. The reforms had not lasted for long. Most recently, a reform mayor, James D. Phelan, had with Victorian tones of righteousness succeeded in revising the City and County of San Francisco's laws, the City Charter. The citizenry saw only moral uprightness in the unmarried Phelan. Yet, on the side, there were affairs with a married woman and a mistress.

Phelan's opponent in the political arena was Abe Ruef. After graduating law school, Ruef had grown his law practice. He had also seen how politics worked in the real world and the most effective way of getting things done—arranging to be paid large legal fees for services that would facilitate approval of construction permits, block legal actions by the opponents of corporations that retained him, and more. Ruef was careful to specify in writing that such payments—fees or retainer—were for legal services. Because he was not a public employee, fees for legal services were not considered a bribe. What was suspected by many, but not obvious, was the splitting of those fees with others. Payments were given to his own personally chosen candidate for mayor, as well as through third parties to those in a position to approve projects for Ruef's clients: some members of the San Francisco Board of Supervisors, the city's "legislature," that had authority to approve or vote down all projects or agencies that required funding.

San Francisco's political fixer, Ruef, didn't look like a lowlife. The "Curly Boss" was always a natty dresser. His bow tie was in place, crisp and fresh. Unlike New York City Tammany Hall's "Boss" Tweed decades before, San Francisco's "Boss" wasn't physically large, but slight of build, with curly hair and a well-trimmed mustache grown in his youth for distinction. Early on, he really hadn't been a bad guy at all.

Abraham "Abe" Ruef, the only son of a Jewish family that had left France in 1862, was born in San Francisco two years later. This San Francisco native son was brilliant. At age eighteen, he graduated from the University of California, Berkeley, with honors. He moved on to Hastings School of the Law in his hometown and was admitted to the California Bar when he was only twenty-one.

Prospects were bright. His father had done well with the dry-goods store opened after the family arrived in San Francisco. He had invested the profits in real estate. Ruef senior's profession was listed as "capitalist" in city directories. The family attended a prestigious synagogue.

Abe Ruef spoke several languages, had studied art and philosophy, and had been passionate about politics, even in his university days. Ruef and several college-student friends founded the Municipal Reform League to study corruption in the existing political system and what could be done to change it. When his law studies were finished in 1886, the young man looked for a place to practice law and develop his interest in practical politics and reform.

The times were politically turbulent.

Most California politics were effectively controlled by the Southern Pacific Railroad, the same corporation that had used legal cases enforced by federal US marshals to ensure its land grant rights to sell land adjacent to its track. (One attempted enforcement resulted in the bloody Mussel Slough incident in 1880—see Chapter 9.) Through Charles F. Crocker, the Big Four capitalists who owned and controlled the Southern Pacific Railroad (SP) had the say-so on who could run for office in California and who couldn't. The SP controlled appointments for both major parties—Phelan's Democrats and the Republicans Ruef would become involved with. No political operative would become powerful without the consent of the SP and the also-influential public utilities.

At the most basic political level, there were precincts to be fought for. Parties and factions were organized as clubs that were under the umbrella of a county committee. There, control was exercised by a leader, someone who could speak to higher-ups and had a degree of authority. The most powerful operative in a local organization was a boss, whether he or the organization acknowledged it or not. Some bosses were labor leaders, some small businessmen, some, like Ruef, had legal backgrounds. The clubs held municipal conventions before an election to choose leaders and approve a platform; seldom were there challenges to the prearranged choices for either.

How did Ruef, a reformer-idealist lawyer just out of law school in 1886 turn into his polar opposite, a conniving political puppet master?

Ruef saw a newspaper notice about a Republican club meeting and decided to get his feet wet. Two men were present, not a crowd, and they told Ruef that they had been elected during the meeting that had just ended. One man asked if he could write and dictated what Ruef, in his enthusiasm, believed and wrote up as a glowing account of meeting details where more than one hundred people had participated. Ruef's rendition was published in a newspaper the next day. He later realized that he had been fed a line, but one Republican Party club faction realized that his polish and skills could be useful. And he had just become old enough to vote for the first time.

Within two years, a leading Republican boss asked Ruef to get involved in the organization. Others pointed out that an ambitious lawyer would want to get to know the judges in town who also happened to be elected through the political party system Ruef was being asked to join. He was hooked.

For Ruef initially, being a Republican Party operative, however minor, meant running precincts in North Beach, San Francisco's "Latin Quarter." It required personal participation as well as donations to organizations and causes. Long hours paid off. Favors were given and releases were arranged for those arrested. The tax assessor's office, coroner, and others might cooperate to benefit a Ruef client.

In 1892, Democratic reformers won power, and by 1896, Phelan, wealthy from his father's fortune and his own banking and real estate investments, was elected, promising to continue the reforms. One issue was the decades-old City Charter, which vested decision making only in the board of supervisors that could fail to take action if the group was fractious. Phelan proposed a new City Charter that placed the mayor in a position to guide and direct the board of supervisors.

What was good in theory, the mayor as a strong executive, played into Ruef's hands when Mayor Phelan blundered in handling a major labor strike in 1901. Unionized teamsters and others working along the waterfront protested against a contract awarded by employers in violation of its closed shop—use only our workers—provision. Non-union men were hired by employers and were labeled "scabs" by the teamsters and their supporters. Phelan directed the police to protect the non-union drivers and a riot ensued.

Ruef, already starting to organize his own Union Labor Party outside the mainstream Republican Party, seized the opportunity. He would run his Union Labor candidate against the Democrats and Republicans in a three-way race, splitting the vote, perhaps in his man's favor. Ruef settled on a personal and union client, Eugene Schmitz, the musicians' union president, with whom he had also had business dealings. Schmitz was tall, dark-haired, handsome, German-Irish and Roman Catholic. He was also a union official, union member musician, band leader, and employer of others. On all counts, especially his looks, Ruef told Schmitz, he could make him a winner despite Schmitz's lack of education and knowledge of city business. In a few days, Schmitz agreed. When he spoke at the Ruef-manipulated Union Labor Party convention in 1901, his Ruef-written speech and Schmitz's delivery gained him the nomination.

Most organized labor supported Schmitz, who was coached and had speeches written by Ruef. As businessmen and real estate investors, the duo, with Schmitz as front man, claimed to know how to deal with business. Ruef later recalled that he spent $16,000 of his own for campaign halls and trappings, while the mayor would ironically only receive a $6,000 salary for serving his two-year term. The mayoral preparation, wooing of labor, reassurance to the business community, and Ruef's campaign expenditures paid off: Schmitz won handily. Afterward, the two men secretly went to Sonoma for Schmitz to be briefed on city matters by Ruef. The lawyer-kingmaker had even greater ambitions. Ruef envisioned Schmitz in higher office and himself as a US senator.

The new 1901 administration, for which Ruef served as the unsalaried attorney for the mayor's office, made the Schmitz-Ruef connection obvious to all. Ruef wrote the mayor's speeches and official documents and conferred with those wanting help, meeting late into the night at his favorite restaurant, The Pup. He listened to all, helping where his influence could help. The Pacific States Telephone and Telegraphy Company representative offered to pay Ruef a cash retainer for being available to answer questions about municipal law, in actuality, asking for help quashing franchise competitors. Accepting, Ruef crossed an ethical line.

Without the support of a majority of supervisors whose votes decided policy, Mayor Schmitz made grand gestures of apparent reform of the Board of Health and Police Commission and vetoed publicly unpopular budget provisions. Schmitz travelled to New York to speak on behalf of congressional candidate and owner of the *San Francisco Examiner,* William Randolph Hearst, met

President Theodore Roosevelt, and spoke at labor conventions in New Orleans and Los Angeles.

Ruef worked behind the scenes to ensure that the next election would give the Schmitz administration, and himself, more control. Ruef allied himself with William F. Herrin, chief counsel and political strategist for the Southern Pacific Railroad, which favored Republicans. Ruef's power-brokering ensured that the SP-preferred incumbent gubernatorial candidate would win re-election in 1903. The Schmitz ticket won again in 1903.

One newspaperman had long hoped for a continuation of Mayor Phelan's reforms and a clean city regime with Schmitz's election in 1901, but quickly clashed with Ruef. The crusading managing editor of the *San Francisco Bulletin,* Fremont Older, had sent Schmitz a letter warning him against associating with Ruef. With the letter made public, an upset Older began a campaign to battle what he believed was corruption with his stories of the administration's and Ruef's alleged graft. Older went, as he later described it, "doggedly in pursuit." Ruef and his supposedly corrupt mayor-henchman were receiving or larding out "boodle," bribe money.

With a second term in 1903, the Schmitz administration had more appointments to make and a board of supervisors that could be influenced with fees shared by Ruef from his clients' retainers, given out through an intermediary. Smelling the stink of corruption, influential men, including former Mayor Phelan, were ready to back an investigation that would gather evidence against the mayor and his right-hand man, Ruef.

One sensational case involved a Chinatown building at 620 Jackson Street that Older charged was a brothel, built after the city demolished an "unsanitary" opium den. The Standard Lodging House had a suspicious number of rooms and traffic. The *Bulletin* charged that police were raiding and closing other houses of prostitution to eliminate competition for what he dubbed, "The Municipal Crib." Older got the grand jury and district attorney to visit, and more than seventy women were arrested. The alleged building owners got a restraining order; finally, personal observation by the presiding judge concluded that "a continuous stream of people [were] going in and out." Years later, Ruef revealed that he got one-quarter of the profits and split the amount with Schmitz.

French restaurants in San Francisco were widely known to be proper dining establishments on the ground level, often with private dining rooms or private dining and bedrooms on floors above. The issue of liquor/wine license renewal for the French restaurants was subject to approval or denial by the four-member police commission. Ruef offered to run interference with recalcitrant members of the commission on the restaurant owners' behalf—for a fee, which he may have split with Schmitz, who personally urged the commissioners to approve the renewals. In the end, Schmitz fired one commissioner on a morals issue to accomplish the goal.

An obsessed crusader, Older at the *Bulletin* continued his campaign against Ruef, his stories taking on the tone of vitriolic modern-day editorials. Ruef, along with former newsboy Mayor Schmitz, engineered a newsboy strike that effectively stopped distribution of the *Bulletin* for a short time.

An opposition group formed for the 1905 election that wanted to curb Schmitz's growing power. It secretly included the SP, a Democratic Party boss, an organization of employers, and others considered anti-union because they advocated an open shop without unions. This fusion group was guided by Older but was too fractious to beat Schmitz's personality-filled, rally-the-troops campaign style and Ruef's behind-the-scenes maneuvering. When the 1905 election results were in, Schmitz had been re-elected and supervisors that Ruef felt he could control with payoffs even though he didn't know many of them personally had swept into office. Ruef was boosted up on the shoulders of supporters and carried down Market Street that was then and now San Francisco's main street.

The month before, in October, the Committee of Twenty of the National Board of Fire Underwriters had issued a report on potential fire hazard in San Francisco. Although the water supply would be enough for demand, the report noted that fire in the city's large number of wooden buildings had been prevented, so far, by a vigilant fire department, but that the potential for fire was "alarmingly severe." No one thought that one of San Francisco's traditional perils, an earthquake, might lead to major fires. The report was ignored.

One San Franciscan, Francis J. Heney, a US attorney general's office special assistant and special prosecutor, stated publically that he personally knew that Ruef was corrupt. Challenged by Ruef, Heney could not produce evidence. With point man Heney willing to take on Ruef through the legal system, Older, Phelan, and another millionaire who had been offended by Ruef's offers to arrange city matters, Rudolph Spreckels, persuaded Heney that a graft prosecution could and would receive financial support. The graft prosecution group also enlisted the famous investigator William J. Burns, on leave from the US Secret Service, as a private detective to follow Ruef and find out about his activities. Evidence gathering began in early 1906.

Ruef was aware that he was being investigated but did not take it seriously, having previously forced Heney to admit there was no evidence.

Nature intervened with the massive earthquake of April 18, 1906. Buildings toppled. In the next three days, fire, spread further by dynamiting to create a firebreak, torched much of what was left. The Pearl of the West was left a smoking rubble heap, with skeletons of poorly built public buildings revealing shoddy cut-rate construction, and a hopelessly inadequate water supply as the Fire Underwriters had warned.

Mayor Schmitz dealt with the aftermath, and Ruef continued deals and behind-the-scenes politics. Crime increased and the corrupt police department couldn't control thefts and assaults. Ruef, on water company retainer, pressed city officials to approve his favored water system, opposing the Phelan-supported Tuolumne Hetch-Hetchy water project that would bring a permanent water supply to San Francisco from Yosemite in the distant Sierra

Nevada. Supporting candidates picked by the SP, Ruef hoped to maneuver himself ever closer to a senatorship.

One of Ruef's nominees for office was William H. Langdon, who as district attorney turned out to be strict in rooting out illegal gambling and slot machines, surprising Ruef. New supervisors started spending money well beyond their means or supervisorial pay. After the earthquake, Schmitz took a tour of Europe in high style beyond *his* means that led many to charge the corruption was blatant. The graft investigation team finally enlisted District Attorney Langdon, then campaigning for governor, who agreed to make Heney an assistant district attorney. On October 20, 1906, Langdon's announcement of a formal graft investigation appeared in the newspapers.

Older got the presiding superior court judge to impanel a new grand jury of men not influenced by Ruef. When there was a break between the drawing of all nineteen grand jury names, Ruef summoned the acting mayor and others to his office and demanded that District Attorney Langdon be replaced immediately. Ruef was appointed in his place, and immediately ordered Heney's discharge as assistant D.A. The battle had begun.

In the year of the Great Earthquake and Fire, the public was restless and demonstrations were held outside the temporary Superior Court chambers in the Temple Israel synagogue. The legality of Langdon's replacement was challenged, and finally, after a statement by California's attorney general that he would appoint Heney as his assistant (to prosecute Ruef) if Ruef wasn't removed as district attorney, the graft prosecution began.

The five joint Schmitz-Ruef indictments finally filed by the grand jury on November 15 charged that the two men were guilty of extortion of money from three French restaurant owners. The two men retained separate legal teams. At arraignment, Ruef first refused to stand up, then stood with his back to the judge. Legal maneuvers followed.

Ruef pleaded "not guilty." His lawyers tried to get a writ of habeas corpus from a presumed-sympathetic judge on the basis that the indictments were flawed and Ruef could not be prosecuted. Ruef disappeared after being freed on bail and failed to appear in court. First the sheriff, then the coroner, could not locate Ruef. Tipped off by detective Burns, a specially appointed court officer, William J. Biggy, took Ruef into custody. Ruef's allegations of judicial prejudice were refuted and his extortion trial began on March 13, 1907.

In the meantime, the graft prosecution team set up a bribe scenario for the supervisors. The supervisors took the bait and the majority were persuaded to give sworn statements about past bribes they had received from Ruef's operatives. The supervisors were promised immunity from prosecution if their testimony didn't waver. So, on March 18, Ruef faced sixty-five additional indictments for bribing supervisors.

Faced with exposure, Ruef asked for complete immunity in return for a recitation of what he had done. Heney was adamantly against it. Burns attempted to persuade Ruef to confess. Meetings and wrangling continued. The bottom line was that Heney was unwilling to grant Ruef immunity without knowing in advance exactly what Ruef's testimony would be. If the evidence was sufficient—perhaps ensnaring SP officials or others—Ruef might get off. Two rabbis acted as go-betweens and told Ruef that for an admission of guilt, immunity was guaranteed, their understanding of Heney's instructions. Eventually, Ruef said in court that he was not guilty, but would change his plea to guilty.

The boss was asked for details of payments and was called by the defense in Schmitz's trial, but to everyone's surprise, not by the prosecution, because Heney did not trust Ruef to testify truthfully. The jury found Schmitz guilty of extortion, and he was legally required to resign as mayor. Schmitz was sentenced to a five-year term in San Quentin.

With San Francisco's civic administration under fire, the mayor and most supervisors were replaced by men hand-chosen by Phelan, Spreckels, and Older under the Progressive movement banner then represented in Washington, DC, by President Theodore Roosevelt.

One small group of operatives had replaced their Ruef-Schmitz nemesis with its own loyalists.

Ruef and his testimony were kept on hold by Heney who was determined not to call him to the stand for the prosecution of transportation and utility company attorneys and representatives. The boss was in limbo, having pleaded guilty but not yet tried or let off under an immunity agreement.

On January 9, 1908, Schmitz's conviction was invalidated by the district court of appeals on a technicality: that the elected mayor or anyone else could ask or threaten to withhold brothel liquor licenses and would not be guilty of extortion. On March 9, the California Supreme Court agreed and said further that the indictment had not named Schmitz as mayor or Ruef as a political boss. Schmitz, still popular with many union members, still faced bribery charges.

Ruef's trial on charges that he influenced the board of supervisors with bribes on behalf of United Railroads, a trolley company that paid him a retainer to endorse their overhead line to replace San Francisco's cable cars, finally began on November 6, 1908. A disgruntled, rejected juror and ex-San Quentin inmate shot Heney in the head on November 13. In jail the next night, the man committed suicide, despite having been searched when booked. Police Chief William J. Biggy, responsible for the jail and police guards, was hounded by the graft prosecutors, newspapers, and citizens groups, and after taking a boat ride across the bay on a foggy night, fell overboard and was discovered dead weeks later.

Ruef's trial resumed and on December 10, a jury took five ballot votes before returning Ruef's and the graft prosecution's only bribery conviction out of 383 indictments issued in the graft cases.

In 1910, despite a detailed and wordy account of everything that had transpired, the district court of appeals denied Ruef's appeal. The California Supreme Court Justices' signatures granted a rehearing, but it was later pointed out that the chief justice had signed the document before reviewing the evidence in the case. On this technicality, Ruef finally entered San Quentin on March 7, 1911, without further case review.

Abe Ruef (right) on the steps of San Francisco Superior Court
COURTESY SAN FRANCISCO HISTORY CENTER, SAN FRANCISCO PUBLIC LIBRARY

Fremont Older had changed his mind. He disliked the graft prosecution team's tactics and Ruef's single conviction for conditions rife in San Francisco and elsewhere: buying influence. He began an immediate campaign in the *Bulletin* for Ruef's parole in the minimum time legally permitted. Ruef's personally written memoirs were published in the *Bulletin* as, "The Road I Traveled: An Autobiographic Account of My Career from University to Prison, with an Intimate Recital of the Corrupt Alliance between Big Business and Politics in San Francisco." Older visited Ruef in San Quentin and they became friends. After an intense effort spearheaded by Older, Ruef was paroled on August 21, 1915, and in January 1920, he was pardoned.

Older went on to rehabilitate San Quentin prisoners, while continuing to write for the newspapers and campaign for causes. Ever-popular Eugene Schmitz ran unsuccessfully for mayor but was finally elected to several terms as a San Francisco supervisor. And Ruef? He managed his real estate and offered ideas for city development and reform but never again dabbled in politics.

SOURCES

University of California Professor Walter Bean wrote the hard-to-put-down *Boss Ruef's San Francisco* (Berkeley: University of California Press, 1952), partially based on Ruef's later memoirs. It remains the definitive reference for the era's city politics and Ruef's career and fall. *My Own Story* by Fremont Older (San Francisco: The Call Publishing Co., 1919) was written by the anti-corruption crusader and newspaper editor who explained his shift from Ruef chaser to an advocate for the boss's pardon. Charles F. Adams's chapter on Ruef, "The Kingmaker Who Put the City up for Sale," in *The Magnificent Rogues of San Francisco* (Palo Alto, Calif.: Pacific Books, Publishers, 1998), labels Ruef a "frightening conniver," and details the history of his machinations.

The Great Earthquake and Firestorms of 1906 by Philip L. Fradkin (Berkeley: University of California Press, 2005) weaves the Ruef-Schmitz corruption with a description of earthquake events and the civilian and military response to San Francisco's great disaster. *California: A History of the Golden State,* by Warren A. Beck and David A. Williams (Garden City, New York: Doubleday & Company, Inc., 1972), provides a good summary overview of corruption and the Progressive political and economic era that followed the graft trials. *Fire & Gold: The San Francisco Story,* by Charles A. Fracchia (Encinitas, Calif.: Heritage Media Corporation, 1996) presents a quick, concise summary of San Francisco's history from Sir Francis Drake's 1579 visit to the California coast to the 1989 Loma Prieta Earthquake. Ruef's history and trials are included in this coffee-table-size browsing book, appealing for photos not seen in other references.

Kevin J. Mullen, San Francisco deputy police chief when the White Night Riot occurred on May 22, 1979, to protest the manslaughter verdict given Dan White, the ex-supervisor who shot Mayor George Moscone and gay Supervisor Harvey Milk, delved into the police archives for *The Toughest Gang in Town: Police Stories from Old San Francisco* (Novato, Calif.: Noir Publications, 2005). The "What Really Happened to Chief Biggy" chapter mentions possible police graft in the department during Chief Biggy's era that spanned the Schmitz mayorship, and the very suspicious and mysterious nighttime disappearance of Biggy overboard in San Francisco Bay in November 1908.

CHAPTER 12

Labors Framed
Framing Tom Mooney for the 1916 Preparedness Day Bombing

Often enough, the person who seems to be the jerk goes to the slammer while the people who put him there are the real jerks. One such man was Tom Mooney, a labor organizer, impolitic, impassioned, likely to rub people the wrong way with what he said and wrote. In all those things, Mooney wasn't a standout. But the incident at the 1916 Preparedness Day Parade in San Francisco that got him framed made Mooney a poster boy for how bad guys create a scapegoat, make it stick, and ruin a life.

This is the tale of Thomas J. Mooney, known as Tom Mooney, who wasn't guilty of murder. His friend and associate, Warren K. Billings, wasn't guilty of murder either. They were framed. It is set in a nervous era when a foreign war is on the horizon, labor is restive in Los Angeles and San Francisco, politics on the left are socialist to anarchist, and the average man-on-the-street has a vague concern about domestic terrorism that is frequently whipped up by politicians and the press in the name of patriotism.

In the unsettled year of 1916, blame is likely to be pinned on the persons most likely to have committed the crime, even if evidence is less than solid. It's a decade so in turmoil that in the case of Mooney, San Francisco's own attorneys will ensure a conviction even if they have to have a witness who will perjure himself. No one can save the framed men unless some California governor is persuaded to pardon the two convicted criminals.

Here is Fremont Older, the crusading newspaperman who helped the graft prosecution nail boss Abe Ruef for corruption a few years before. He has lived to regret it and tries to rally support for Mooney and Billings where he believes justice has miscarried. It is a tale of easy scapegoats who are set up and sent down to prison and of the jerks and the system that put them away...

San Quentin Prisoner #31921 was leaving his cell for the last time. Tom Mooney smiled and breathed, a free man for the first time in twenty-two years. It was January 7, 1939.

Since he had been incarcerated, the Great War, as World War I was then known, had bloodied the trenches of Europe. The United States had raced through the Roaring Twenties and was now finishing a wallow through the Great Depression. Soon there would be another war, but in the meantime, Mooney was free, triumphant.

His appearance was very unlike his Death Row mug shot taken on July 17, 1918. Then, a meticulously inscribed chalkboard had sat beneath the shaven-headed Mooney's chin, beneath the thin, unsmiling line of his lips:

31921
THOMAS J. MOONEY—AGE 35
MURDER 1ST DEGREE = DEATH
SAN FRANCISCO NAT. ILL
TO BE EXECUTED AUG 23, 1918
7-17-18

In five weeks he had been due to die.

He hadn't committed the crime for which he was sentenced to capital punishment, nor had Warren Billings. Billings was still in Folsom State Prison in January 1939. Mooney and Billings had been framed, for what they were—labor activists with histories— and for what they represented in America—leftist politics and occasional acts of murderous violence in the name of union rights.

It had all gone so wrong almost two years to the day before Mooney's Death Row photograph was taken.

San Franciscans had joined a country being psychologically readied for possible entry into the war already engulfing Western

Thomas J. Mooney
COURTESY SAN FRANCISCO HISTORY CENTER, SAN FRANCISCO PUBLIC LIBRARY

Europe. A Saturday afternoon Preparedness Day Parade down Market Street from the Ferry Building was announced for July 22, 1916. "Peace through Preparedness" and "March of the Patriots," the notices around town had urged. New York City's Fifth Avenue Preparedness Parade had been on May 13, a template inspiring other cities to organize similar orderly patriotic demonstrations. This was serious business in a city like San Francisco where many laborers actively disagreed with any attempt to involve the country in a foreign war. Nothing in San Francisco's parade felt celebratory except for the flag in almost every spectator's hand.

The crowd of thousands lined the sidewalks several feet deep behind a phalanx of policemen along the curb. Most waved small American flags. There were more spectators hanging out of windows and from balconies of the buildings along the Market Street parade route. It was warm for a San Francisco summer day, and Tom and his wife, Rena Mooney, a music teacher with a studio in the building, had gone up to the roof of the Eilers Music Company Building at 975 Market Street (a long block west of the Fifth and Market Street cable car turnaround) for a good view of the parade. They watched, with others, from a spot more than a mile west of the Ferry Building, the customary starting point for parades. During the parade, the Mooneys were photographed inadvertently by someone on an adjacent roof taking amateur pictures from the high vantage point.

The contingents of parade walkers were orderly, preparing to march in rows like military brigades. The Grand Army of the Republic (Civil War veterans), Spanish-American War veterans, businessmen, women (who did not yet have the right to vote), and others were included, but no union or labor groups. Labor unions were widely known to be opposed to involvement in the European War.

The parade scheduled for 1:00 p.m. had gotten started about 1:30 p.m. so that Market Street could be cleared of vehicles and the police line set. Leading off as grand marshal was Thornwell Mullally, a United Railroads director who had put down strikes by car men, another reason why labor unions weren't included in parade plans. The crowd cheered when Mayor "Sunny Jim" Rolph followed Mullally. Dapper dresser James J. Rolph Jr. was popular and had hosted the world at San Francisco's Panama-Pacific International Exposition the year before to prove to the world that San Francisco had risen like a phoenix from the ashes of the Great 1906 Earthquake and Fire.

Unlike the exuberant parades for the 1915 exposition, the Preparedness Day crowd kept a respectful silence as rank upon rank of marchers passed by. Some in the newspaper buildings around Third Street knew that a few days before, there had been "direct action" mentioned or threatened in hand-written notes delivered to the newspapers, business people, and the Chamber of Commerce Law and Order Committee. Later, several reporters commented on the "tense" atmosphere.

The marching groups started from a staging point on Steuart Street (where today one can dine at One Market Restaurant). It was one block west of The Embarcadero where the Ferry Building tower stood at the end of Market Street. At that corner was the Ferry Exchange Saloon. Some people were outside the drinking establishment watching the groups forming up. Several noticed a brown suitcase by the wall that a few people recalled may have been put there by a man about 1:30 p.m. Within a few minutes, one of the older Grand Army veterans had collapsed from heat prostration, been helped out of the way by friends, and was awaiting a police-summoned ambulance.

The Grand Army of the Republic and the groups that followed began moving toward the corner of Market Street at 2:04 p.m. By 2:06 p.m., the Spanish-American War veterans were approaching the corner. An explosion, later determined to be from the saloon wall area where the suitcase had been placed, flung the veterans and watchers, including some children, up to fifty feet away, with body parts later found at twice that distance.

Few people reacted, since it had been announced that a cannon blast in Mullally's honor would signal that the crowd would sing the "Star Spangled Banner." As loosened building glass rained down on the crime scene and the smoke started to clear, the bomb site carnage was revealed. Police Captain Duncan Matheson, who was in charge of blowing his whistle to start each group on the parade route, started organizing ambulances. In spite of the chaos, a Spanish-American War captain ordered his bleeding men to "March!"

Police Lieutenant Stephen Bunner began organizing body covering and keeping looters away. The injured were put into trucks to be taken to hospitals. Bunner wasn't a detective and didn't investigate, mark body locations, collect evidence, or take down names of witnesses. When the casualties were gone, Bunner had another policeman attach a fire hose to a hydrant and wash the blood and residue away. Whatever evidence there may have been to identify the bomb maker or bomb assembly was gone. Including the collapsed veteran, there were ten dead and forty injured by the blast.

Spectators saw the veterans limping and bleeding, continuing the march up Market Street. The newspapers quickly got telephoned reports and sent ace reporters out to find scoops. San Francisco *Bulletin* editor Fremont Older who had spoken out against preparedness "nonsense" at a meeting two days before worried that he might get blamed for something. About 3:00 p.m., the Mooneys heard from a policeman who had come up on the Eilers Building roof that bombs were being thrown off downtown roofs.

At 3:30 p.m., the district attorney arrived at the explosion crime scene. San Francisco's district attorney, Charles M. Fickert, had been elected by San Francisco voters in 1909, defeating Francis J. Heney, the graft prosecution lawyer who as assistant D.A. had had Boss Ruef sent to San Quentin. Fickert was a central California rancher's son from modest circumstances who had graduated from Stanford University and was primarily known for outstanding college football feats. Adding a law degree, he had represented both labor groups and corporations. He was not known for intellectual brilliance but was well-connected socially and politically through Stanford University alumni ties and marriage. United Railroads supported his candidacy for district attorney.

With Fickert was the California Bankers Association secretary, Frederick Coburn. Coburn found a hammer and enlarged bomb-created holes in the pavement and wall, finding bullets and some fragments. Photographers were allowed to take pictures that showed the enlarged holes. By now, the crime scene had been cleared of bodies and body parts, hosed down, and physical damage increased. At 4:30 p.m., Police Captain Matheson ordered the area secured and put under guard. No one had called detectives. Law enforcement officials and prosecutors had failed to do even a basic "CSI"—crime scene investigation.

With a terrified San Francisco populace, the newspapers duked it out. They accused one another and most of the graft prosecutors and anti-union leaders of committing the crime. The focus quickly shifted to anarchists, widely believed to advocate violence, including bombings, to achieve change. Anarchist-atheist Emma Goldman had been in town to lecture on anarchism, birth control, and against preparedness patriotism. Alexander "Sasha" Berkman, who had been imprisoned years before for an assassination in New York, was publishing an anarchist paper, *The Blast,* in San Francisco. The whereabouts of Goldman and Beckman lunching together at the time of the event was corroborated.

Other anarchist groups' headquarters were raided by the police and produced only reams of literature.

Who, then, had planned and executed the Preparedness Day bombing?

More than $15,000 was put up as a reward by government and private sources, much more than was eventually given to bombing victims and their families. *The New York Times* wrote that such a large amount of money encouraged authorities to look around for the real criminal, but that they would be pressured to convict someone.

The focus shifted to those who had been involved in violence in the past or who had a reputation for knowing about explosives. Labor activists were among those who seemed to fit the profile. The names included Tom Mooney and Warren Billings.

Tom Mooney, the son of an Irish-American coal miner and labor organizer and Irish immigrant mother, was born in Chicago in 1882. Tom's labor activities were that of an organizer or steward, not a labor official or local officer. With only a few years of education, he began working at fifteen as an iron molder's apprentice. By nineteen he was a member of International Molders' Union, and had been denied journeyman status by his employer. Cycling through jobs at foundries, Mooney began organizing workers to protest low pay and uneven male-female workloads. His reputation made potential employers shy away.

In 1907, he had saved enough money to sail to Europe and explore art museums as he traveled from country to country absorbing culture. A chance encounter with a Socialist in a Rotterdam museum led Mooney to spend the rest of his trip looking at workers' lives and working conditions. Back in Stockton, California, in 1908, he joined the Socialist Party of America, throwing himself into selling party literature and speaking. There he met music teacher Rena Hermann, who he later married. In 1908, Tom and his brother John Mooney campaigned for Eugene V. Debs, the Socialist Party candidate for president of the United States. After the unsuccessful campaign, Tom started a course of self-study, his "education." In late 1909, Mooney briefly joined and spoke on behalf of the Industrial Workers of the World (IWW) in Wallace, Idaho, in support of free speech and against the banning of political street meetings in Spokane, Washington.

By 1910, Mooney was back in San Francisco, his base for visiting California's labor strongholds to gather subscriptions to the Socialist Party's *Wilshire Magazine*. He came in second in a subscription-selling contest and was awarded a trip to the International Socialist Congress in Copenhagen, Denmark. Rubbing shoulders with the Socialist elite made Mooney more determined to work for industrial unionism where all workers were unionized together (as opposed to skilled crafts workers who were represented by the AFL, the anti-socialist and much more conservative American Federation of Labor).

That was the year when anti-union activity shifted into even higher gear. In the early hours of October 1, 1910, the Los Angeles Times building was bombed, killing twenty-one people. It infuriated the newspaper's anti-union owner and Los Angeles booster Harrison Gray Otis. He had shepherded anti-picketing provisions into a local ordnance and had helped make Los Angeles an open shop city. Labor organizers, brothers James B. and John J. McNamara, were quickly arrested.

Tom Mooney was involved in the defense committee's San Francisco efforts. But two months after the McNamara trial began, their famous defense attorney, Clarence Darrow, told the court that his clients were changing their pleas to guilty. In an apparently brokered deal, the McNamara brothers were sentenced, but in the end, not paroled as promised. There was talk of a frame-up. Labor reeled, and labor leaders became reluctant to support defense funds.

Mooney's own fights were with other unionists, about organizing, use of funds, strike actions, and how the average members were treated. His comments were adamant and didn't permit disagreement. The language was forceful, critical, and alienating.

Mooney was in charge of picketing a San Francisco shoe factory in 1912.

Intending to go south to join Pancho Villa's revolution in Mexico, nineteen-year-old New Yorker and skilled shoe cutter Warren Billings had paused in Oakland. Billings started looking for temporary work in San Francisco and met Tom Mooney. When Mooney asked, Billings was willing to act as a strikebreaker in order to identify the actual strikebreakers. Mooney got run over by the factory owner and Billings got beaten up by company guards. After the strike ended, Mooney invited Billings to live with Rena and him while the young man found new employment. They became friends.

Labor strikes targeted another major Bay Area company, the Pacific Gas & Electric Company (PG&E) utility. Dynamite was often used to disrupt service along the lines at the transformer points. Billings agreed to take a suitcase with unknown contents from San Francisco to Sacramento. He took public transit to the saloon drop-off point and was confronted by Sacramento detectives with guns and by Martin Swanson, then with the Pinkerton Detective Agency, accompanied by PG&E's property agent. Opened, the suitcase revealed sixty sticks of dynamite. Billings was tried for carrying explosives on a public conveyance and was sentenced to spend two years in Folsom State Prison.

Mooney and two electrical workers were arrested about the same time on charges of having dynamite, guns, and parts for bomb assembly in a skiff the three had left at a wharf not far from the Carquinez Strait. There, PG&E had transmission lines that fed power to the area, and company officials were worried about sabotage. However, a deputy sheriff had previously found the empty boat. Mooney and the others later testified that the skiff had leaked and that they had gone into town to get repair materials. Two hung juries and an acquittal later, they were freed. Mooney was then re-arrested as an accomplice in the Billings Sacramento suitcase incident, a charge that was dismissed for lack of evidence. Pinkerton detective Swanson was fired when it was established that he had framed three union men in a dynamite plot. He was immediately hired by PG&E.

Mooney baldly criticized everyone from AFL leaders, local labor officials, and Utah's governor who refused to pardon labor activist and singer Joe Hill, who was shot by firing squad. California Governor Hiram Johnson he labeled a "cowardly cur."

Mooney's next organizing foray was against United Railroads, San Francisco's municipal transit company. Mooney, his wife, and associates were watched, and their move to hand out leaflets and call the car men out on strike was thwarted. Rena Mooney was arrested. San Francisco's attention was quickly diverted by the June 1, 1916, Pacific Coast Longshoremen's strike that closed the ports and resulted in violence and death. Billings returned to the city after his release from Folsom Prison.

One day, jitney driver Israel Weinberg, who knew the Mooneys and sometimes drove them to events, picked up Swanson as a fare.

PG&E's Swanson offered Weinberg money to set up a business elsewhere if he would testify that Mooney had participated in yet another bombing of power transmission lines in nearby San Bruno not long before. Weinberg refused and was threatened with removal of his jitney driver's license. Swanson approached Billings with the same offer. He said he'd consider it and immediately told Mooney.

Billings and the Mooneys knew they were being followed. Suddenly, on July 19, the surveillance seemed to disappear, but they anticipated another move by Swanson. Billings dropped off a camera for the Mooneys who had planned to go on a short vacation, a Russian River camping holiday delayed in the end by a relative's arrival for the weekend.

On July 21, the San Francisco Labor Council issued a resolution noting that because organized labor was opposed to preparedness that "an attempt may be made by the enemies of labor to cause a violent disturbance during the progress of the parade and charge that disturbance to labor." If that happened, the statement said, it would be a "frame-up."

On Preparedness Day during the parade, the Mooneys were watching from the Eilers Building roof. Billings was near Union Square working a small sabotage job that would force car owners to have expensive repairs done at an automobile dealer. Weinberg spent the day driving his jitney around downtown, being blocked by the police phalanx as the parade prepared to start.

District Attorney Fickert met Martin Swanson on the night of the bombing. When Swanson left Fickert's hotel room, he had been hired as the D.A.'s "special investigator into the bomb cases," head of a bomb squad to find the perpetrators. Police Captain Matheson, a street officer but not a detective, was appointed the Bomb Bureau's head investigator.

The following Wednesday, with Fickert present, Swanson identified Billings as Billings was waiting to go into a previously scheduled hospital appointment. Billings was arrested but not told the charge. Weinberg's jitney was halted by police, and he was arrested, but the arresting detective did not know the charge. Swanson and his team searched Rena Mooney's studio and gathered literature, correspondence, revolvers, and cartridges while the Mooneys were camping along the Russian River. There were several other arrests, including Edward Nolan, in whose garage Tom Mooney stored his motorcycle. Only one search or arrest warrant had been issued—for the Mooney studio—but its paperwork was not handled legally.

On Thursday, the *San Francisco Chronicle* noted that dynamite suspect Thomas J. Mooney was being sought by police. The Mooneys saw a newspaper with the headlines and started back to San Francisco. They were arrested at a train stop and taken back to the city, questioned separately, and denied legal counsel.

A young woman, Estelle Smith, was produced by Fickert. She identified Billings as the very nervous man with a very heavy-looking bag who had said he was a photographer and wanted roof access to the office building where she worked on Preparedness Day. The location was three-quarters of a mile west of the bombing site.

All five, the Mooneys, Billings, Weinberg, and Nolan, were separately called before the Grand Jury that had already heard testimony from witnesses presented by District Attorney Fickert. Not all witnesses who had come forward testified, and not all evidence gathered by the Bomb Bureau was introduced. Tom Mooney and Billings refused to testify because they had not been allowed to see an attorney. Rena Mooney testified, and Weinberg and Nolan, who had seen counsel briefly, also did. On August 2, 1916, all five were indicted on eight counts of first-degree murder.

Billings was tried first. Jurors were not selected at random but came from a pool of regulars with known backgrounds. The assistant district attorney urged the jury to convict but to sentence Billings to life in prison, rather than execution. Billings's defense attorney had closed his argument to the jury, saying his client was chosen as the first to go to trial because he would be the easiest to convict and that the prosecution had then gone out to find supporting evidence. To the shock of almost everyone, the jury did just that. Jurors later remarked that Billings's alibi for his whereabouts just didn't hold up. Suddenly, witnesses who had been interviewed by the prosecution but not called to testify and had information that did not place Billings at the crime scene began contacting the defense legal team. Those witnesses said that they had reported what had happened at the parade. One woman had been visited by Swanson who urged the witness to testify against Billings anyway, to help her husband keep his job. On October 7, 1916, Billings was sentenced to life imprisonment at Folsom State Penitentiary.

Tom Mooney was next. The trial began on January 3, 1917. Some of the witnesses who had testified against Billings were discredited. The defense presented photographs that showed the Mooneys on top of the Eilers Building and clocks in the background that showed the time. Then, the prosecution called Frank Oxman, a "wealthy cattleman from Durkee, Oregon." The detailed story told by Oxman was believed, the tale of a businessman who said that he had noticed details because he had a cattle ranch and it was his business to notice things. Under cross-examination, Oxman testified that he had written down such details as jitney driver Weinberg's license plate number and type of vehicle because the accused had all been acting nervous. Oxman added that he thought the jitney might have been stolen. The calm cattleman's detailed account blew the defense apart.

On February 9, the jury delivered a guilty verdict. A few days later, Mooney was sentenced to be sent to San Quentin for execution on May 17. An appeal was filed.

In the meantime, Fremont Older was told that Oxman, indeed an Oregon cattleman, had conveniently decided to testify for D.A. Fickert's defense and brought in a man from his hometown of Grayville, Illinois, to back up his story. That man, Oxman, Estelle Smith, and the other prosecution witnesses had Fickert's and his assistant's assurances that there would be plenty of reward money to go around if they testified to seeing Mooney and the others acting during the Preparedness Parade. The Grayville man refused, and later used his information and receipts to prove that Oxman had not been in San Francisco on the day of the parade, could not have witnessed the events, and had been suborned to perjure himself. Oxman was tried on perjury charges but acquitted.

Defendants Rena Mooney and Israel Weinberg were tried but eventually acquitted. Nolan, considered a minor player, was never tried.

Mooney and Billings had been framed. Mooney's labor activism, prior accusations of being involved with bombings, a righteous but abrasive manner, and ambitious politicians stacked the deck against him.

The Bolshevik Revolution brought demonstrations in "Muni's" favor in Russia followed by marches in much of Western Europe. The pressure was on the United States and President Woodrow Wilson to act.

The California Supreme Court upheld Mooney's conviction in March 1918, with execution scheduled for August 23. The stark Death Row photograph of prisoner 31291 was taken.

Charles Fickert was affirmed in office after a recall election soon after mysterious bombings occurred at the governor's mansion.

President Woodrow Wilson's Mediation Committee conducted a 1918 investigation of the Preparedness Day cases in San Francisco that concluded that justice had not been done. Wilson wrote to California Governor William Stephens requesting that he consider mercy. Labor demonstrations were held throughout the country in July, on "Mooney Day." The governor commuted Mooney's sentence in early August, but he remained in prison.

For twenty years, Mooney, his defense committees, and his supporters tried to get him a new hearing, stymied by legal procedures that would not permit a new trial. Mooney was so adamantly hands-on with his defense that he sometimes lost chances for legal appeals.

President Herbert Hoover appointed a National Commission on Law Observance and Enforcement (known as the Wickersham

Commission), that used an investigation of the Mooney case as an example of "lawlessness in law enforcement." In 1932, a sanitized report was issued, omitting sections "Suppressed by the Wickersham Commission" that were later privately published. The suppressed report concluded that the police investigation was actually only a search for conviction evidence; the arrests, lack of arraignment, denial of counsel, and unlawful searches violated the law; witnesses were never required to identify defendants in a police lineup; the trials were conducted in the press as much as the courtroom; the prosecution concealed witness credibility evidence; witnesses were coached "to a degree that approximated subornation of perjury"; and that subsequent attempts to free those convicted were minimized "by a campaign of misrepresentation and propaganda carried on by those officials who prosecuted them."

On January 7, 1939, Mooney left San Quentin. After only five days in office, California's new governor, Culbert L. Olson, had unconditionally pardoned Mooney as his first official act. In October, the California Supreme Court agreed to Governor Olsen's request that it act on Warren Billings's pardon. On October 17, Billings left Folsom State Prison, his sentence commuted but still short of a full pardon.

Bad prison food had always aggravated Tom Mooney's stomach. For most of the three years he lived after the pardon, he was sick and hospitalized. When he died in 1942, Mooney, ever the activist, was chairman of the Citizens' Committee to Free (Communist Party USA general secretary) Earl Browder.

SOURCES

Frame-up: The Incredible Case of Tom Mooney and Warren Billings (New York: W. W. Norton & Company, Inc., 1967), by author and former newspaperman Curt Gentry is dedicated to W. K. B., Warren Billings, whom Gentry knew personally and liked. Gentry's in-depth research tries to show beyond any doubt that Mooney could not have exploded the bomb, and the "Whose Bomb?" appendix runs through evidence and possible culprits. Another detailed work in readable, narrative form is Richard H. Frost's *The Mooney Case* (Stanford, Calif.: Stanford University Press, 1968).

In *The Gentle Dynamiter: A Biography of Tom Mooney* (Palo Alto, Calif.: Ramparts Press, 1983), a Mooney activist and one-time newspaperman and CIO official, Estolv E. Ward, combines a search through Mooney's voluminous papers that were bequeathed to the Bancroft Library and contemporaneous newspaper articles with his own memories of Mooney late in life. Ward analyzes the events swirling about Mooney and the personalities of Mooney family members.

The Mooney-Billings Report: Suppressed by the Wickersham Commission was privately published in 1932 (New York City: Gotham House, Inc.), revealing government investigators' conclusions of justice system abuses in the Mooney case.

An excellent summary of the *Tom Mooney Trial: 1917* is in *Great American Trials,* edited by Edward W. Knappman (Detroit: Visible Ink Press, 1994).

After the Preparedness Day bombing, many San Franciscans saw a silent film that the Library of Congress Motion Picture, Broadcasting and Recorded Sound Division preserves as *San Francisco's Future* (http://hdl.loc.gov/loc.mbrsmi/lcmp003.48888). Partially animated, the film appeals to patriotism with San Francisco's rebuilding from the earthquake and fire rubble, and to paranoia with a choice of prosperity raining coins down on the city or a burning city with a title card warning: ANARCHY, SEDITION, LAWLESSNESS.

CHAPTER 13

Loans for a Teapot
Edward Doheny, Oil, and the Teapot Dome Scandal

A century ago, in 1912, petroleum became so strategic that a US president designated special oil fields to be permanently protected against private exploitation. Then, as now, oil policy affected everyone, from oil companies and investors to an individual driver watching prices escalate at the local gas station.

Two presidents later, a posse of jerks infested the early 1920s administration of President Warren G. Harding. The jerks created a scandal with oil whose name became synonymous with corruption at the highest level. Late in the 1920s, the Teapot Dome congressional investigation and criminal trials revealed the Harding era's laissez-faire attitudes toward handing off lands in the public trust to private entrepreneurs for exploitation. There was influence peddling. Some transactions reached the criminal level.

Among the bad guys investigated and tried for the Teapot Dome offenses, one got caught. Another Los Angeles man's skilled lawyer and importance to American national defense got him legally exonerated from charges of conspiracy to defraud the US government and of giving a bribe. This is the story of the second man, California's oil baron from Los Angeles, whose friendship with the first man and their monetary transactions enmeshed them both in one of the twentieth century's most significant scandals.

The Teapot Dome scandal required eight trials, with seven defendants who were charged with six types of crimes. The accused were tried over five years, from 1926–1930. President Harding's secretary of the interior received a total of $404,000 from oil barons, presumably to throw his support and authorization to them in the purchase of oil leases for three naval petroleum reserves. California's oil magnate, Edward Doheny, stood trial twice. Doheny's one son and only heir was the messenger boy, carrying money to the interior secretary.

Edward Doheny said he loaned the money to help his old friend, Albert Bacon Fall, to help Fall pay for a beloved ranch in New Mexico. A "loan to an old friend" it may have been, but Interior Secretary Fall was in a position to do something sweet for Doheny in return, a very lucrative favor.

In some eras, there is a general atmosphere of corruption. After World War I, Americans, including ever-optimistic Californians, heaved a sigh of collective mental relief. The strictures and belt-tightening required by US participation in The Great War were over, the soldiers were back home, and even though it looked like President Woodrow Wilson's League of Nations wasn't going to get support at home after all, the War to End All Wars should have taken care of disputes. The nation turned away from worry about the future and concentrated on having more fun and getting rich *now*.

But just in case there might be a future national emergency, the US Navy Department had fought hard to get several permanent petroleum reserves set aside in 1912. Petroleum extraction had become practical by the turn of the twentieth century, and fortunes had been made from finding, drilling, and exploiting the petroleum resource. Oil, "black gold," had replaced coal as fuel on steamships and for transportation. Automobiles, too, used mostly petrol (gasoline) once Henry Ford rolled out the mass-produced Model T in 1909. America's oil dependence had begun.

The savvy men who could find and extract that oil made fortunes. One such man was Edward Doheny, who hailed from Wisconsin. He worked for the United States Geological Survey (USGS) in Kansas and the Black Hills of South Dakota, learning about mining, metallurgy, and geology. In the 1880s, while still in his twenties, Doheny landed in the last region of the United States where the Wild West still held out, the Arizona and New Mexico Territories. Men wore guns and carried rifles to settle disputes. It was a place where a man could take on cattle thieves and protect mining claims while prospecting for gold, silver, or other minerals.

Irish-American, Catholic, and poor, Doheny had graduated high school at fifteen, worked various jobs, and then at age eighteen had learned about Western geology while working for the USGS. He went freelance to try mining. His reputation in the Southwest was that of a smart man who could defend himself and his mining claims. While in New Mexico, he met a business partner, Charles A. Canfield, and became friends with another man who was already working mining claims: Albert B. Fall.

Fall, from Kentucky, was five years younger than Doheny. Mostly self-taught, he had worked on a farm, as a cowboy, and had invested in mines in Texas and New Mexico. New Mexico became his home and he taught and practiced law there as well as prospecting on his claims. With a lawyer's reputation for defending notorious murderers, Fall eventually became a New Mexico Supreme Court judge. In that position he became notorious himself for personally riding out with a posse. Elected to the New Mexico Territorial Legislature in 1898, Fall served as an infantry captain in the Spanish-American War. Fall had his eye on a ranch at Three Rivers, New Mexico, that was to become his pride and joy—and downfall.

In 1892, Doheny, who hadn't held on to any of his New Mexico mining profits, followed Canfield to Los Angeles where his partner had succeeded in real estate. Whether a true story or legend, the standard lore has Doheny in a Los Angeles street in 1892 noticing that a wagon being driven by an elderly African American contained thick black goo. When he asked the driver what the stuff was, already suspecting that he knew from his geological training, the man said *brea,* or pitch, that was being used as fuel.

Doheny knew that that meant petroleum. He found out where the *brea* was coming from and arranged to lease the land. He used a pick and shovel to start, then devised a eucalyptus tree

trunk drill to finish the shaft at the corner where Glendale Bou-
levard and Colton Street intersect today, in the Echo Park area
(not far southwest of Dodger Stadium). It was a gusher. Doheny
and Canfield quickly developed several hundred more oil wells in
downtown Los Angeles, among 2,500 or so oil derricks that were
soon pumping around town, day and night. The partners, as Pan
American Petroleum and Transport Company owners, invested in
oil exploration and extraction in California's Central Valley, elsewhere in the United States, and in one and one-half million acres
around Tampico, Mexico. Doheny created a private army of six
thousand petroleum field guards for his Mexico oilfields, where
gushers were described as exploding like volcanoes, sending
equipment and land flying into the air. To protect his Mexico interests, Doheny sided with one Mexican president, then another—
any president who would back Doheny's oil interests—and tried
to influence American presidents to support Mexican leaders who
permitted Doheny's company to drill and extract oil.

Doheny even persuaded California's powerful Southern Pacific
Railroad to switch from coal to petroleum-based fuel oil, got road
builders to use petroleum in mixing asphalt, and lobbied the US
Navy to convert the fleet to oil power.

Doheny quickly became a multimillionaire. His lifestyle
reflected it. He and his second wife, (Carrie) Estelle Doheny, lived
in the Doheny Mansion in a residential Los Angeles neighborhood
developed by Doheny. He built his only son, Edward L. Doheny Jr.,
known as Ned, the Greystone Mansion in Beverly Hills. The elder
Doheny doted on his five grandchildren by Ned.

Ned Doheny had been raised by his stepmother, Estelle, after
his parents' divorce, mother's suicide, and his sister's death. He
had graduated from the University of Southern California. He was
groomed for the family petroleum business and, as World War I
loomed, was active in the California Naval Militia. In 1917, he was
called to active duty on an armored naval cruiser, where fellow
officers wrote their families that Doheny, son of privilege, hated
duty on a vessel. Edward Doheny arrived on board and spoke pri-

vately to Ned's commander. Soon after, Ned was transferred to shore duty in the judge advocate's office in Washington, DC, in a non-legal capacity for the rest of the war. After his military service, Ned returned to Los Angeles and the family business, his social life, his clubs, and philanthropy.

Back in 1912, two years after Doheny's first Mexican gusher began convulsing seventy thousand barrels of oil per day, President William Howard Taft's executive order had established three naval petroleum reserves. Reserve No. 1 was 38,989 acres in the California Central Valley's Elk Hills. Reserve No. 2 was nearby in Kern County, and the smallest, Reserve No. 3, was under Teapot Dome in Wyoming. In that year, the US Navy Department and the secretary of the navy were given sole control over the strategic public lands removed from private sector development. Doheny had his eye on Naval Petroleum Reserve No. 1.

In the same year, 1912, Fall became one of the new state of New Mexico's US senators. His sentiments matched Doheny's: use public lands by letting private companies exploit the resources. Doheny and other oilmen spoke to the navy and members of Congress about possible drainage from national petroleum reserve oilfields that could deplete the resource by bleeding the petroleum into neighboring, privately leased fields. The oilmen's expertise was generally accepted, although drainage was never a proven issue. The US Navy and President Woodrow Wilson's administration resisted all pleas to lease the naval petroleum reserves. Only the navy selectively drilled on the reserves for petroleum to boost its own limited supplies in storage depots.

That all changed when the new Warren G. Harding administration took power in 1921. Harding, an Ohio Republican newspaper publisher and senator, had been the reluctant but inoffensive compromise presidential candidate. He brought some old friends with him to fill cabinet posts, and those friends recommended New Mexico Senator Albert B. Fall for secretary of the interior. Fall meshed well with the Harding cronies from Ohio, cabinet secretaries, and others with whom the president would privately play poker and defy Prohibition laws to drink bootleg whiskey several times a week.

Early in the administration, Harding's executive order on May 31, 1921, moved control of the naval petroleum reserves to the secretary of the interior, Fall, who had urged Harding to do so. The action was supported by the secretary of the navy who had heard what he considered persuasive arguments from Edward Doheny over the years that the private oil companies should be allowed to drill to prevent reserve drainage. The change horrified navy officers who said it would be dangerous to let Big Oil use and profit from the nation's emergency oil supplies.

Looming in the background was a need to build more navy fuel oil depots with storage tanks, especially in the Pacific at Pearl Harbor, Hawaii. Since 1913, the law had required the navy secretary to request an appropriation for new fuel storage facilities. Congress had never agreed to fund Pearl Harbor, an expensive undertaking.

In 1921, Fall arranged for the navy to receive naval petroleum reserve lease royalties in paper certificates instead of in cash sent to the Treasury Department where those funds were no longer available to the navy. The certificates could be used to buy what the navy needed: oil storage. This way, Fall explained to the navy secretary, the navy would directly benefit from the dollars earned by the leases.

Doheny, who had already acquired a few Elk Hills leases, was one of few oilmen who could afford to build Pearl Harbor storage. But his complaint to his friend, Interior Secretary Fall, was that the royalty pricing on his few existing Reserve No. 1 leases—already fixed by competitive bidding—was too expensive. Fall promised to authorize additional Elk Hills leases at lower cost—if Doheny built at Pearl Harbor.

On November 28, 1921, Edward Doheny wrote Secretary Fall a formal offer to build Pearl Harbor storage tanks in exchange for the all the unrefined oil extracted from the California naval petroleum reserves. With an estimated three hundred million barrels of oil in

Naval Petroleum Reserves No. 1 and No. 2, Doheny's potential oil profit could have been as much as $300 million, a huge sum compared to the costs of constructing the costly Pearl Harbor facility. Doheny's note was the sole "bid" for the oil leases and the Pearl Harbor project. Notably, there was no attempt at putting either project up for competitive bidding.

Early on November 30, Fall picked up the telephone and placed a call.

Drought during the early twentieth century had parched the Southwest. Albert Fall's ranch at Three Rivers needed improvements. By the time he had become secretary of the interior, Fall had not paid property taxes for ten years. An Albuquerque newspaper owner who had clashed with Fall many times over the years noticed the ranch's run-down state and unkempt appearance. Fall also wanted to acquire the neighboring Harris Ranch, which held rights to water on both properties. Fall had no sources of ready cash to pay back taxes, to fix up Three Rivers Ranch, or to buy the Harris Ranch that was on sale for about $100,000. Fall had discussed leaving public life for a post in the petroleum industry as others, including his predecessor, had done.

Over the years, various friends and business acquaintances, including one partner-industrialist in Cleveland and Henry Ford Sinclair, president of the Sinclair Consolidated Oil Corporation, had offered to help Fall out with ranch costs. Edward Doheny was later to call his old friend Fall his "Pard[ner]."

The call Fall made on November 30 was to Edward Doheny. Fall said he was "prepared now to receive that loan." The money, to be in cash, not a check, was for the Harris Ranch purchase. Fall later said that the money transfer was a business matter and that they had agreed that Fall would pay back the $100,000 from his salary when he left the government to work for Doheny's oil operations.

Interior Secretary Albert Fall's phone call to Doheny came less than two days after Doheny's formal written offer to build Pearl Harbor storage in exchange for reserve leases.

Edward Doheny called his son, Ned, then in New York with Ned's private secretary-bodyguard, Hugh Plunkett. The father told his son to go to their investment banker and withdraw $100,000 in cash from Ned's own account. Then Ned was to deliver the money to Fall in Washington, DC

Ned and Hugh took the train, delivered the bag with the cash, watched Fall count it, and took Fall's IOU receipt. There was no interest rate, payment period, or terms on the IOU note. Ned and Plunkett returned to New York. Fall immediately left for New Mexico and purchased the Harris Ranch with cash. Within a few weeks, Henry Sinclair had come to visit Fall at Three Rivers and was assured that he could lease the Teapot Dome Reserve. Sinclair offered to send Fall livestock that Fall said he couldn't afford.

Back in New Mexico, neighbors and newspapermen soon noticed that the Three Rivers Ranch had been fixed up, complete with the (Sinclair-) promised cows and a thoroughbred racehorse; that Fall now owned the Harris ranch for which he'd paid $100,000; and that all back taxes had been paid.

Final naval petroleum reserve lease contracts with Doheny and Sinclair were signed in 1922; the only other bids either proposed to build only part of the Pearl Harbor storage complex or questioned the legality of public lands' leasing and lack of naval and Congressional consultation and consent. Fall "accepted" Doheny's and Sinclair's bids for the three naval petroleum reserves in 1922.

Official Washington was becoming aware that the naval petroleum reserves and other resources were being allocated to private businessmen under suspicious circumstances. There were calls for an investigation.

On March 4, 1923, Fall resigned and left for his Three Rivers Ranch. Often unwell, Fall intended to take a short break before joining Edward Doheny's oil operations. While on a tour to Alaska and the western United States, President Harding died suddenly in San Francisco on August 2. Calvin Coolidge, the new president, had been silent throughout Harding's cabinet meetings. Coolidge may have known what had been going on, although he denied it. Public outcry for an investigation was strong and growing.

On October 23, 1923, the Senate Committee on Public Lands and Surveys began its investigation. Progressive Montana Senator Thomas J. Walsh questioned Fall, who cited the Fifth Amendment, and refused to incriminate himself. Edward Doheny's testimony confirmed a $100,000 loan to Secretary Fall, with only the IOU promissory note as evidence of the arrangement. Fall's signature had been torn off the IOU. Doheny mentioned that his wife Estelle had torn the signature off but maintained that the cash had not been a bribe and that there was no profit for him in the lease projects.

Bipartisan co-special counsels were appointed by President Coolidge: Owen J. Roberts and Atlee W. Pomerene were to help the committee and prepare court prosecutions. Roberts, who ended his career as an associate justice for the US Supreme Court, was the lead prosecutor. They were aided by a Secret Service investigative team.

The Senate hearings and detective work proved that Fall had spent several hundred thousand dollars to make Three Rivers Ranch improvements and buy the Harris Ranch, which his interior secretary salary couldn't justify. With enough evidence to go to court, Roberts wanted to get the public property back. He filed civil suits in 1924 against oilmen Doheny and Sinclair to get the naval petroleum reserve leases cancelled and back into government hands. Both men were charged with fraud. Roberts won his case against the California magnate, and won on appeal against Sinclair.

Roberts was ready to act. The first Fall and Doheny trial for a *criminal* conspiracy to defraud the government began in late 1926, the first of eight trials for Fall, Doheny, Sinclair, and several other defendants. Doheny's attorney was Frank J. Hogan, a famous, self-made trial lawyer who was famous for announcing, "The best client is a rich man who is scared." The rumors were that Hogan commanded a one million dollar legal fee for his services.

The Dohenys, father and son, were worried. Ned, the money messenger, had not been involved in the naval petroleum reserve discussions with Fall and others, yet Ned had also been indicted.

The first criminal trial began with jury selection on November 22, 1926, in the Supreme Court of the District of Columbia. It was Roberts for the government against feisty, eloquent Hogan for the Fall-Doheny defense.

Hogan gave his passionate summation to the jury:

Do you think that a man who left his home at the age of sixteen and followed the trails of the pioneer West, who dug in mother earth for the minerals hidden therein, who with pick and shovel sunk wells that he might bring out the gold and the liquid that today mean safety for worlds, would, even if he himself could, stoop so low as to bribe an official of his government, the friend of his youth and his former days, would, if he could, stoop so low as to bribe an Cabinet officer of the United States of America in order that he might swindle and cheat the land that had given him plenty?

Hogan reminded the jury of the major upheavals of World War I. Ned sat beside his father and Hogan pointed to him:

That old man offered that young man's life on the altar of patriotism. He went on the ships of war over the turbulent and submarine-infested oceans in his country's service, the only son, the only child. And you are asked to believe that when Edward L. Doheny, near the end of his life, corruptly intended to bribe Albert B. Fall, a Secretary in the Cabinet of Warren G. Harding, he deliberately and purposely used as an instrument therefor his son, the pride of his youth, the hope of his maturity, the solace of his old age!

The defense summation also invoked Doheny's "crucifixion," like Christ's, nineteen hundred years before. Finally, the ghost of the late President Harding was called from his Marion, Ohio, tomb. Hogan continued to the jury:

I stand his splendid figure before twelve of his fellow men
and from his resting place I quote his words.

The words were Harding's letter approving Fall's handling of the reserves' leases.

After more than nineteen hours of deliberation, on December 16, the jury returned with the verdict, "not guilty."

Doheny was not to get off completely. The Doheny leases had been executed with fraud and corruption, ruled the US Supreme Court on February 28, 1927. Fall had colluded with Doheny and Doheny had corrupted Fall, a government official when he paid him money, the erstwhile loan. The unanimous ruling held that fraud cancelled any profits Doheny might have made from building the Pearl Harbor storage tanks.

The other trials continued. Fall and Doheny's separate bribery trials were the last on the docket for late 1929 and early 1930.

Unexpectedly, the Los Angeles Police Department was summoned to Ned's mansion, Greystone, on February 17, 1929. Ned and Hugh Plunkett were dead in the same suite of rooms, with Ned lying in his own blood. There was a Colt .45 nearby. Murder? Murder-suicide? The evidence did not add up, and no one has ever proven who might have killed the two men. Edward Doheny, summoned not long after the discovery, wept on the floor over his son's body.

Albert Fall stood trial in October, charged with accepting Doheny's bribe. Always in poor health, for this trial, Fall was in a wheelchair. Hogan made reference to acquitting Fall before he was summoned to the "Great Beyond," but the jury found him guilty. He served nine months and nine days of his one year prison sentence but was never able to pay the $100,000 fine, the equivalent of the amount of the bribe.

By March 1930, the Teapot Dome scandal had its last criminal trial. The defendant was Edward Doheny, charged with giving Fall, a government official, the bribe that Fall had been convicted of receiving. Doheny looked much older at age seventy-three than he had been when the investigations began more than six years before. Hogan cited Doheny's patriotic spirit and pulled at the jury's emotions:

> *Do you believe this man is a crook? If he's a crook, then convict him. But can you believe his mind was so corrupt that he conceived bribery and that he had fallen so low that he selected his own son, whom a few years before he had given to the navy, as the instrument of his bribery? Ned Doheny says to you from the grave that which in life he said from this very witness stand. The indictment charges that young Doheny was a briber. Can you believe that? Can you believe that a man who a few years ago had offered his only son to his country had fallen so low that he took him, the expected solace of his old age, and made him into an instrument of bribery? It isn't human to believe that.*

The jury believed Doheny's lawyer and acquitted the oilman.

In the end, one man got nailed for his crime and did his time. Fall, the first man, was convicted of accepting a bribe that the second man, Doheny, was acquitted of having offered and given.

It was only money to Doheny. Edward Doheny refunded $34,981,449.62 to the US government under the court-ordered Elk Hill lease cancellations. If money means influence, and influence means power, and power can corrupt, Doheny's actions in the Teapot Dome scandal may be those of an ultimately acquitted but driven-to-succeed jerk.

Sources

M. R. Werner and John Starr used congressional hearing testimony, trial court records, newspaper stories, and US Secret Service documents to prepare a very readable account of the *Teapot Dome* scandal, including the actions of the Dohenys and attorney Frank Hogan (New York: The Viking Press, 1959). M. R. Werner included a shorter version in his close-to-contemporary book, *Privileged Characters* (New York: Robert M. McBride & Company,

1935), noting that the 1920s and Harding period had witnessed the country's second worst display of government corruption to date (after the Ulysses S. Grant administration), as demonstrated by hearings and trials.

In *The Origins of Teapot Dome: Progressives, Parties, and Petroleum, 1909–1921* (Urbana, Ill.: University of Illinois Press, 1963), J. Leonard Bates, an associate professor of history at the University of Illinois, realized that no one had written about the conservation, politics, and regionalism pertaining to oil and petroleum policy in the two decades before the scandal broke: He wrote the "backgrounder." Business, financial, and political writer Laton McCartney wrote *The Teapot Dome Scandal* (New York: Random House, 2008) in an entertaining narrative that mines the hearing testimony and profiles the Teapot Dome personalities and their family members with an evocative subtitle: *How Big Oil Bought the Harding White House and Tried to Steal the Country.*

Robert Grant and Joseph Katz included Teapot Dome among *The Great Trials of the Twenties: The Watershed Decade in America's Courtrooms* (Rockville Centre, New York: Sarpedon, 1998). *Great American Trials,* edited by Edward W. Knappman (Detroit: Visible Ink Press, 1994), provides an excellent short summary of the events surrounding the eight Teapot Dome trials.

CHAPTER 14

Movie Morals

Roscoe "Fatty" Arbuckle and the Hays Code

One night in San Francisco changed a big man's life forever. The fall from grace of a beloved Hollywood actor was both dramatic and tragic, with long-lasting effects for him and for his industry. The big man, a comic genius, was condemned as a jerk for reports of his extracurricular behavior. He was tried as a criminal, and thus as a major jerk, for the purported deed. Three juries didn't convict him. But Hollywood studio men did. So did their censorship board and its head operative. The chief movie morals mogul made sure the highly paid comedian didn't work. For a long time, the big man was box office poison.

The story of Roscoe "Fatty" Arbuckle, cast as a jerk, and his undeserved downfall from success, is a morality tale of one man sent into a tailspin by the real jerks in Hollywood who destroyed his livelihood and his life.

The actor is graceful, acrobatic, but weighs in at upwards of 260 pounds. He moves deftly on his feet for such a large man, as lightly as Fred Astaire, someone will say. His larger-than-life funny man character in silent films is both solicitous of his leading ladies and oblivious of what's happening to them. There, his slightest movement, pratfall, or bow is magnified by the silent black-and-white film's flickering high contrast. He's thirty-four years old and has been pleasing audiences since he was twelve. Now, he's a man at the top of his game—entertainment—and the year is 1921.

"Fatty" Arbuckle, the actor smiling on thousands of movie posters, loves to create elaborate practical jokes in real life. He doesn't like that professional name, "Fatty," but unhappily puts up with

Roscoe "Fatty" Arbuckle
FROM GEORGE GRANTHAM BAIN COLLECTION: LIBRARY OF CONGRESS PRINTS AND BAIN NEWS SERVICE PHOTOGRAPHS DIVISION

it for the sake of his career. He has a name, he says: "Arbuckle. Roscoe Arbuckle."

When he was born he weighed thirteen pounds. He grew into huge girth early. Roscoe never blended into a crowd as a youngster growing up in Santa Ana, California. He was just too conspicuous.

Roscoe Conkling Arbuckle was one of the youngest of nine children in his family, with a sometimes drunken and physically abusive father and a mother who died in 1899 when he was twelve. Sent away afterward by relatives, he tried to find his father in San Jose, California, where his dad and an older brother were supposed to be making a good living. Instead, the overweight but likeable boy with a tiny cardboard suitcase, abandoned, had to fend for himself doing chores around a hotel.

Baby-faced Roscoe had size; an acrobat's ability to juggle, tumble, and somersault; a surprisingly fine singing voice; and a good sense of timing. Encouraged by the hotel piano player, he sang and performed in amateur theater evenings. One night, to avoid being pulled off the stage as he was ending his performance, he somersaulted off it in front of the audience. The crowd ate it up.

Arbuckle led audiences in sing-alongs with lyrics projected over the stage. He worked as a singing waiter, dishing out popular and operatic music in San Francisco and performed in vaudeville in the Pacific Northwest. Then he hooked up to be one man of a trio touring rough honky-tonk saloons. One night when the main female singer didn't show up, Arbuckle put on a wig and the singer's clothes and sang her repertoire. When she arrived, he did his classic somersault off the stage to escape and one of his partners pushed the diva off the stage on top of him. It was a crowd-pleaser. Fatty Arbuckle was learning comedy. He was learning how to adapt the sweet, baby-faced large character to many roles, including some in girl's or women's clothing. Arbuckle then spent a summer with a classic theatre company. Through it all, he was watching performances and practicing his own skills and craft.

Minta Durfee, an eighteen-year-old dancing and singing chorus member met twenty-one-year-old Arbuckle in 1908 as she refused his persistent trainside offer to help with luggage. Roscoe was smitten. When her job with their acting company ended and she was leaving, Arbuckle took the much smaller Durfee to the Long Beach Pier and held her upside down over the water until she agreed to marry him. Taking the train home, she was roused by a German-accented man enquiring about her luggage. It was her large suitor. Durfee succumbed. They were married in the Byde-A-Wee theater where they had performed; the public paid admission to attend the elaborate ceremony before the day's show.

On tour soon after, performing *The Mikado* in Japan, Shang-hai, and Honolulu, Arbuckle's drinking made him rude and insult-ing to the hosts. Durfee apologized for Roscoe's behavior, even as fellow cast members squirmed. Durfee, Arbuckle's first wife, was to continue to stand by Roscoe in the bad times in years ahead—and put up with the abusive side of his drinking.

In 1909, Arbuckle did his first film, a "flicker," for Selig Studios. Thomas Edison had been pioneering film technology with educa-tional one-subject short films for several years at his Bronx, New York, Edison Studios. Most actors and vaudevillians thought the new films crude, temporary, and demeaning to their employment value as legitimate entertainers. But the money was becoming too good to refuse in an upstart industry that packed theaters for five cents per head. Arbuckle, like many others, reluctantly followed the money.

The American film industry's original studios were in New York City, New Jersey, Philadelphia, and Chicago. Studio owners quickly found that the cold weather season and ubiquitous urban scenery were limiting. Eventually, almost all studio owners moved opera-tions to Southern California. The film industry first settled in Santa Barbara because of its architecture that harked back to idealized Spanish heritage, and its fine year-round climate. In 1918, filmmak-ers headed one hundred miles south for more varied scenic locations and open space in a part of the Los Angeles basin called Hollywood. Long shooting days in natural light and pleasant climate made for faster film shooting schedules and year-round comfort.

One of those who headed for California in early 1912 was Mack Sennett, whose brand-new Keystone Film Company was to make slap-dash comedies and give its name to a clueless bunch of authority figures, the Keystone Kops. The action was madcap, much improvised from the original idea or gag a writer had fleshed out. One- and two-reelers were ground out from studios using multiple sets or on location. Shooting days were long. Arbuckle began as a Kop, then quickly became an on-screen duo with a well-known comedienne, Mabel Normand. At Sennett's Keystone, he also became "Fatty" Arbuckle, with tent-sized pants, a tiny derby hat, and a blissfully unaware look that made audiences laugh, all for a few dollars a day in salary.

Charles Spencer Chaplin, an Englishman, was hired from the vaudeville stage and joined the Arbuckles and Normand on the Keystone set. Charlie Chaplin's standard melodrama character, a shabby, frock-coated man, was quickly transformed into The Tramp's prototype, with Chaplin using Arbuckle's huge pants, a too-tiny hat, and big shoes from another actor. Arbuckle and the much shorter Chaplin were paired with each other often, one playing the main character in a film, the other, the leading man in the next. After a year of learning the ropes, developing his character, acting, directing, and writing for his films, Chaplin went on to greener pastures at another studio for more than five times the salary. Within several more years, Chaplin was earning one million dollars a year. The Arbuckles, Normand, and others were still performing slapstick comedy with Sennett at wages of about five hundred dollars a week.

In 1915, a feature film, *The Birth of a Nation,* directed by D. W. Griffith, was released, drawing huge audiences into film theaters for an opus that lasted more than three hours. The industry was beginning to see profits in longer productions, with involved plot lines, much more complicated than the Sennett mad chases and pies-in-the-face.

After a trip to New York and New Jersey, with the Keystone contract expiring, in 1916, Arbuckle accepted an offer for complete control of his films at one thousand dollars a week and a one million dollar salary after three years. His new studio was Paramount; the new boss was Joseph Schenck.

Before he could start at Paramount, an infected knee carbuncle threatened the comic with real leg amputation. Pain and distress gave way to calm with draining and a new doctor's prescription. It was for heroin, it was legal, and Arbuckle quickly became addicted. With his reputation for nasty-tell-all announcements during nights of drinking and a new studio contract, Minta and Arbuckle's friends decided to keep the heroin—even though legal—a secret while nursing him. After several weeks of hospital detox isolation, a depleted Arbuckle, having lost one-third of his weight, departed on a cross-country promotional tour in 1917. There was a brief relapse into heroin dependence, but eventually he recovered.

Working for Schenck in New York at a new company, the Comique Film Corporation, a Paramount subsidiary, Arbuckle met someone who would be one of his fellow actors and most loyal supporters, young Buster Keaton. When Keaton, who had performed with his family his whole life, went with Arbuckle's theatrical agent to watch a Comique production, Arbuckle brought him on-camera to be the guy who gets not the pie, but the flour, in his face. Arbuckle mentored Keaton. They made twelve comedies together as Keaton developed his screen style. Arbuckle instructed and Keaton learned everything, from camera work to physical comedy and timing.

Back in Hollywood, Schenck told Arbuckle to buy a house that reflected his fine Paramount salary. The Arbuckles were living separately, but for the sake of appearances, Minta needed to live in the same house. Arbuckle had been dating his Comique co-star, Alice Lake, but not publicly. The Arbuckles entertained in Hollywood, but drinking brought out Roscoe's anger, foul language, and sometimes he lashed out. Yet, he and Keaton continued wrapping up two-reel comedies every couple of months until World War I and Keaton's military service intervened.

When the war ended, audiences were tired of propaganda and patriotic messages the studios had cranked out for the war effort and looked for films to enjoy, movies that showed luxuries people craved and lifestyles to go with them. In 1920, Prohibition took effect, forbidding the manufacture, transportation, or sale of alcoholic beverages. On August 18, 1920, the Nineteenth Amendment to the US Constitution was ratified, and women suddenly had an equal right to vote. Women were shedding their corsets as society was shedding staid behavior. The Roaring Twenties and flappers had arrived, along with speakeasies and easy-to-find alcohol—if you could afford it.

The lax morals shown onscreen made money for the studios while at the same time upsetting the studio heads who saw the same behavior, hushed-up and private, happening with their movie stars. Keeping things out of the press was a challenge; there was money to be paid to keep things and people quiet. Arbuckle's drinking and parties did not endear him to neighbors, studio owners, or producers. The studio men, from keep-a-Bible-in-his-desk Cecil B. DeMille to the Jewish immigrants who, as successful businessmen, had come to investing in nickelodeons and their own theaters from backgrounds as furriers (Adolph Zukor, Marcus Leow), a jeweler (Lewis J. Selznick), a glove salesman (Samuel Goldwyn), a retail pharmacist (Joseph Schenck), a vaudeville producer (Jesse Lasky), and others (among them, farmers, a reporter, and a piano player).

The pressure of making money; running a business by employing actors and crews, technical production, promotion, distribution; and developing dedicated movie theater chains was intensified by congressional calls for regulation of movie content in the public interest. Despite loosening of social standards, there was plenty of room for resentment and backlash. There were calls for censorship, even in Congress. The times were ripe for an incident, for someone to make a mistake too public to cover up.

Arbuckle was working, through Schenck, under contract to Zukor and Lasky, whose Famous Players-Lasky company created a significant part of Paramount Studios' output. By 1921, Arbuckle was making back-to-back features, six days a week. In his off-time, he partied at his elaborately furnished home or in night clubs and tried to blow off steam.

Each Labor Day weekend, Paramount would have stars make personal appearances, meeting and greeting an adoring public. Zukor ordered Arbuckle to appear, but Arbuckle had other plans for a weekend in San Francisco, away from Hollywood and the studio. Keaton had invited him sailing for the weekend, but Arbuckle was determined to go north, having booked three rooms in a favorite San Francisco hotel, the St. Francis.

He drove up from Los Angeles to San Francisco in his new, luxurious Pierce-Arrow automobile, with friends, an actor and director, along for company. Word was out in San Francisco that there would be a weekend party at Fatty Arbuckle's suite after the men arrived on Saturday. The usual cadre of showgirls and wannabe actresses would appear. There would be plenty to drink, gin and whiskey at least—Prohibition was widely ignored. There would be dancing, music on the phonograph, free drinks galore, and it was a holiday weekend. The party began.

Monday evening, the party was over. An actress, Virginia Rappe, appeared injured, sick, perhaps raped. She, and Maude Delmont, an acquaintance who had come to the party with her, were in a hotel room down the hall, recovering. Delmont had had a lot to drink. Rappe had begun screaming at the party. In Hollywood, Rappe's reputation wasn't good. There were rumors of stripping naked when drinking, prostitution, past abortions, and a current need for money. She was good-looking, but, in the phrase of the era, she was trouble.

Delmont was to tell her story of what happened to Rappe at the party—a tale that accused Arbuckle of rape and crushing Rappe's bladder so that it ruptured. When Rappe died a few days later in a sanatorium known for performing abortions for those who could afford it, the doctors there performed an illegal autopsy and determined that her death had been caused by acute peritonitis from rupture of the bladder. Delmont went to the press, charging that Arbuckle had pressured Rappe for sex, dragged her into his bedroom, and that when Rappe started screaming, Delmont had pounded at the door to get in. What she had found, she said, was Rappe on the bed, screaming that Arbuckle had done this to her. Two other actresses initially corroborated Delmont's story.

Arbuckle had returned to Los Angeles for work and was soon summoned to return to San Francisco for questioning. Arbuckle had told the newspapers his version: Everyone had been eating and drinking a little, including Rappe, who became hysterical. The hotel manager and doctor were called while other women had removed her clothes and put her in a bathtub of cold water to calm her down. Then, we took her to another room and got her to bed. The doctor and I thought: indigestion.

Arbuckle was charged with first degree murder and held in the county jail without bail. Movie theater chains immediately pulled Arbuckle features and made substitutions. Arbuckle's salary stopped. His creditors filed for payment for his mansion's furniture and other belongings. Civic, church, and women's groups decried the lax moral standards displayed by Hollywood and its stars. Within a few weeks, Roscoe had become the bad boy everyone loved to despise for indecency.

His attorney advised him to remain silent. No one wanted the illegal alcohol to come up.

Separate grand and coroner's juries charged Arbuckle with the same crime: manslaughter, but not murder, for the application of some force that caused Rappe's urinary bladder to rupture.

In the first trial, defense witnesses testified to being held by and pressured by the San Francisco district attorney's office. Under oath, others recounted Rappe's previous abortions, a daughter born out of wedlock, chronic bladder problems, probable gonorrhea at the time of her death, and her penchant for running around in the nude wildly when drunk. Arbuckle testified calmly that he had tried to help the vomiting actress who he found in the bathroom, had helped her to lie down on a bed, gotten help to summon a doctor, and taken Rappe to another room to rest where he was ordered out by Delmont. Delmont, a prosecution witness, never testified in the trial. The district attorney had discovered her long history of arrests and charges, including bigamy.

Forty-four hours after the jury began deliberating, the trial judge declared a deadlocked panel and dismissed the jurors. Four days later, President Warren G. Harding's postmaster, Will H. Hays, was asked by heads of the Hollywood studios to become chief of a new entity, the Motion Picture Producers and Distributors Association. Before the public's moral outrage against Hollywood became strong enough to shut the industry down, the film moguls would self-regulate.

Will Hays, an Indiana lawyer, as Republican National Committee chairman had gotten Harding elected in a landslide. He knew how to play politics, avoid scandal, make connections such as those with his oil industry client, Harry Sinclair, mediate disputes among administration officials, and establish rules as he had as postmaster general. As a Presbyterian elder, his moral code was considered above reproach. In early January 1922, the year 90 percent of all movies made in the world were filmed in Los Angeles, Hays took the $100,000 per year job. He was hired to rescue the movie industry's reputation, described later that year by a US senator:

At Hollywood is a colony of these people where debauchery, riotous living, drunkenness, ribaldry, dissipation, free love seem to be conspicuous.
—CONGRESSIONAL RECORD 62:9657, JUNE 29, 1922

Roscoe Arbuckle's second trial began a few days before Hays accepted the film czar post. This time, his attorney felt there was no need to put the actor on the stand again. The facts from the prior trial, plus more to discredit Rappe's reputation, should suffice. The result was another deadlocked jury.

A third trial began six weeks later. Arbuckle testified this time; Delmont, the prime prosecution witness, never testified in any of the trials. The jury deliberated for a few minutes on April 12, 1922, then filed back into the jury box. The foreman addressed the court, reading:

> *Acquittal is not enough for Roscoe Arbuckle. We feel that a great injustice has been done him. We feel also that it was only our plain duty to give him his exoneration, under the evidence, for there was not the slightest proof adduced to connect him in any way with the commission of a crime.*
>
> *He was manly throughout the case, and told a straightforward story on the witness stand, which we all believed. The happening at the hotel was an unfortunate affair for which Arbuckle, as the evidence shows, was in no way responsible.*
>
> *We wish him success, and hope that the American people will take the judgment of fourteen men and women who have sat listening for thirty-one days to the evidence, that Roscoe Arbuckle is entirely innocent and free from all blame.*

Six days later, three months after becoming the movie industry's cleanup man, Will Hays issued a statement on Famous Players-Lasky letterhead:

> *After consulting at length with Mr. Nicholas Schenck, representing Mr. Joseph Schenck, the producers, and Mr. Adolph Zukor and Mr. Jesse Lasky of the Famous Players-Lasky Corporation, the distributors, I will state that at my request they have cancelled all showings and all bookings of the Arbuckle films. They do this that the whole matter may have the consideration that its importance warrants, and the action is taken notwithstanding the fact that they had nearly ten thousand contracts in force for the Arbuckle pictures.*

The "ten thousand contracts" meant a $100 million loss to Paramount. The studio heads were willing to make an example of Arbuckle using Hays to enforce an industry morals code. Arbuckle had been blacklisted. In early December, Hays rescinded the ban and Arbuckle went back to work but not under his own name in front of the camera.

Even though Arbuckle was acquitted of any crime, his name remained associated with a sordid scandal. The public had a long memory, so Arbuckle eventually took a turn at directing under another name, then owned a nightclub, and paid back what he owed. He married two more times.

After a film acting hiatus of eleven years, when Jack Warner offered him a role, Arbuckle was ready to leap into talkies. He did so on a sort of probation. To do more than one of the six Warner-contracted films, Arbuckle would have to prove himself to Hays who had issued the Motion Picture Production Code, "A Code to Govern the Making of Motion and Talking Pictures" in 1930, to spell out, item by item, what was acceptable behavior in the movies.

The night he finished the film, Roscoe Arbuckle celebrated his first year wedding anniversary with his wife, Addie, and the successful relaunch of his career. When they got home and settled for the night, Addie asked him a question. There was no reply. The big man was dead.

POSTCRIPT: ACCEPTABLE CONTENT

The Production Code was in place for several years before it was fully applied and enforced voluntarily by the studio owners on themselves, with constant help from Will H. Hays. Commonly known as the Hays Code, it was in effect until 1968 when the Motion Picture Association of America film rating system was introduced. Hays had a thirty-year career as Hollywood's film czar, delighting in his contacts and friends in the movie industry. As the powerful spokesperson for the men who hired him, Hays used the perception that the Hollywood elite were getting away, literally, with murder, to deprive the talented million-dollar funny man, Fatty Arbuckle, of his career.

SOURCES

Two Arbuckle biographies paint the picture of a personality with comic genius who went from the height of fame to become an unemployable has-been actor. Both biographers spoke to Minta Arbuckle, Roscoe's first wife, to "flesh" out the word portrait. *Frame-up! The Untold Story of Roscoe "Fatty" Arbuckle* is by journalist Andy Edmonds (New York: William Morrow and Company, Inc., 1991). In *Roscoe "Fatty" Arbuckle: A Biography of the Silent Film Comedian, 1887–1933* (Jefferson, North Carolina: McFarland & Company, Inc., Publishers, 1994), a well-known silent film pianist, Stuart Oderman, describes Arbuckle's early life, entertainment jobs, dependency, and relationships with his wives, especially Minta Durfee. The flaws and delicate vulnerability of the star are honestly dealt with for a sympathetic portrait of a man with lots of people and circumstances stacked against him. For a view of Arbuckle and Normand at the height of their film fun in 1915, watch *Mabel and Fatty Viewing the World's Fair at San Francisco, Cal* (http://hdl.loc.gov/loc.mbrsmi/lcmp003.33488), in the Library of Congress collection.

The Memoirs of Will H. Hays (Garden City, New York: Doubleday & Company, Inc., 1955), by Will H. Hays, includes his motion picture period as he reveled in his contact with Hollywood's elite. Arbuckle's career or trials are never mentioned in the *Memoirs* by the person responsible for the actor's unemployability. *The Hays Office* (Indianapolis: The Bobbs-Merrill Company, 1945), by Raymond Moley, covers the history of film oversight by the Motion Picture Producers and Distributors of America with a depiction of Will Hays's beneficent handling of everyone connected with the industry; Moley's densely written book is a reference for what happened to Arbuckle in the context of the 1920s movie morals clampdown.

Robert Grant and Joseph Katz included a chapter, "The Trials of 'Fatty' Arbuckle," that concentrates on the legal issues and actions in his cases in their book, *The Great Trials of the Twenties: The Watershed Decade in America's Courtrooms* (Rockville Centre, New York: Sarpedon, 1998).

The history of cinema is entrenched in Southern California. Kevin Starr, historian and former California state librarian, has written a series of books on California history. In *Inventing the Dream: California through the Progressive Era* (New York: Oxford University Press, 1985), Starr traces the film industry's roots and early history in a chapter entitled "Stories."

CHAPTER 15

Klannish in the OC
Anaheim Falls into
Ku Klux Klan Clutches

A very bad thing happened in Anaheim in 1924. Jerks who didn't reveal the truth got elected to Anaheim's city council and took over. In most of California, including the rest of Orange County, voters would have shrugged off the jerks' duplicity, chalked it up to politics as usual, and voted the bad guys out of office at the next electoral go-round if there was an outrage or scandal that could not be ignored.

In 1924 Anaheim, the jerks were secret members of the Ku Klux Klan who had clandestinely won an election. The jerks included a minister who masterminded the takeover. They were all members of a larger movement swelling the numbers of the KKK nationally. KKK members belonged and expected everyone else in the community to belong, too, or pay the consequences. The secretive KKK takeover followed by overt and heavy-handed Klan presence in town was a scandal and embarrassment that begged to be dealt with. Anaheim's citizenry couldn't wait until the next regular election. People had to get their town back.

In an odd variation from KKK racist persecution of African Americans or Mexicans elsewhere in Southern California, Anaheim's klavern, its local KKK chapter, targeted moral laxness in the community. It was a persuasive argument given the social turmoil amid often puritanical and sometimes hypocritical moral high ground staked out by many in the early 1920s. When fully revealed, the secret activities of the Anaheim KKK temporarily tarnished the reputation of an otherwise pleasant and striving Southern California community.

Photo of a man, possibly Dr. Henry William Head, in early Ku Klux Klan robe and hood, photographed for the 1916 pamphlet "The Ku Klux Klan" by Anne Cooper Burton (Los Angeles: William T. Potter Publisher, 1916)

COURTESY SANTA ANA HISTORY ROOM, SANTA ANA PUBLIC LIBRARY

Anaheim wives were telling their neighbors: Look for the American flag placed just so in the store where you shop. Why not? It sounded patriotic. The men, their husbands, wouldn't go into a place of business where that flag wasn't in evidence, either. Quietly, there were murmurs here and there about a meeting, you know, to talk about those people who drink, even though Prohibition, oh, what a great relief, is the law of the land. And then, there were those Catholics whose people did who knows what with the children they taught. Brainwashing, maybe worse. It was all scandalous!

Not much notice was taken when fiery crosses burned in front of houses in other parts of Orange County, in Fullerton and Yorba Linda. Someone had gossiped that there was a cross burned here in Anaheim. That was maybe true, maybe not. That was the method everyone knew the Hooded Order used to scare folks, maybe some black people or those Mexicans, but it's mostly us white folks here.

It's 1923, for heaven's sake! Though there's been some mention of the KKK, that Ku Klux Klan group, in the *Orange County Plain Dealer* in February. It was something about a church meeting visitor giving money to the church and redressing wrongs and the right people being in charge. Well that was probably just something Pastor Myers, that wonderful man of God at his First Christian Church of Anaheim, sponsored just to make sure everyone knew that he was welcoming everybody when he preached.

Why, just last Sunday night, May 10 it was, he told us all about how the Catholic Church is after him and is going to drive him out of Anaheim. That's because he's exposed how those Catholics may be controlling Anaheim's newspapers, local storekeepers, the civic clubs, why even the chamber of commerce. And, he's always talking about how we all should be "dry," and not allow those bootleggers to get away with selling that liquor, luring people of easy morals to iniquity. . . . Praise the Lord we have our pastor! Reverend Myers is so upright, a model of morality. . .

Reverend Leon Leroy Myers had become Exalted Cyclops, the president of the Anaheim Klan klavern, not long after it formed the second time in late 1922. He didn't make that fact public, even though all over the country, the second iteration of the Ku Klux Klan was publically recruiting members in droves.

The original Ku Klux Klan was concocted in 1866 by Confederate army veteran friends in Pulaski, Tennessee, just as the resented post–Civil War Reconstruction was beginning. Differing accounts mention the Pulaski men dressing up in long robes made from sheets with headgear that covered the face for a burning-off-steam ramble around town at night. What the costumed men hadn't counted on was African Americans' reaction: White ghosts, their former masters, were out to haunt them. Lighthearted silliness quickly became deadly serious.

The KKK, its members disguised with white robes and hoods, grew quickly in the Deep and Upper South. Among methods used to terrorize blacks into leaving communities and intimidating them not to go to the polls to vote were lynchings and warnings to "get out or else!" with crosses set aflame near black homes. In reaction to KKK violence, the Civil Rights Act of 1871, known as the Ku Klux Klan Act, used federal troops to enforce laws against violators that the states couldn't or wouldn't enforce, including prosecution of Klan members.

Orange County's own "founder," the man who advocated separation of the southern portion of Los Angeles County into a separate county with more local control, had also been a member of the original KKK. Dr. Henry William Head, a Santa Ana physician, had arrived in Anaheim about 1876, and been a California state assemblyman for six years representing the area that with his bill became Orange County. Head told pamphlet writer Annie Cooper Burton in 1916 that he had once been a Klan Grand Cyclops in Tennessee in the early years. When she asked, Head produced a wide-collared robe and head covering from his three years of Klan involvement in the late 1860s. Burton's pamphlet published a purported picture of Dr. Head wearing the Klan clothing.

After more than forty years, the Klan was resurrected in 1915 by Georgian William Joseph Simmons. He created and codified Klan-specific terminology. Secretive membership rituals, including phrases to recognize other Klan members, emulated those of popular fraternal organizations that protected groups of workers and people with like interests. Members wore distinctive white hoods and robes for klavern meetings and certain activities. That year, D. W. Griffith's film, *The Birth of a Nation,* had been shown in cinemas throughout the country. Based on a best-selling 1905 novel, *The Clansman,* the gripping narrative glorified klansmen as white women's chivalrous saviors. On Thanksgiving night, 1915, Simmons, self-anointed Klan Imperial Wizard and fifteen followers made the Klan's revival official. They hiked up Atlanta's Stone Mountain and set a cross on fire, mimicking a scene in Griffith's film.

For the next few years, the country was enmeshed in the Great War. In the aftermath of World War I, society struggled with where African Americans and Catholic European immigrants who were moving to the larger urban centers fit into the post-war social order. The KKK advocated a society that was white, Protestant, morally correct, and 'dry' (teetotaling). Women, freed from corsets into looser clothing, had to be careful not to be labeled loose women and a threat to morality if they did anything outside the norm. In 1919, the Eighteenth Amendment to the Constitution established what many social reformers had been pushing for, prohibition of the manufacture, sale, or transportation of alcohol. The KKK advocated strongly for Prohibition and attracted members. States and localities went officially dry, with no legal alcohol. Anaheim had its own tradition to overcome first.

In 1857, German immigrants moving to Anaheim planted vineyards and produced wine until the phylloxera louse–blighted vines ended the dream in the 1870s. Many communities voluntarily became dry in the early twentieth century, but Anaheim's German heritage had never treated alcohol as inherently wrong. Anaheim's proximity to thirsty oil field workers also kept alcohol available until Prohibition. For KKK "reformers" like Reverend

Myers in Anaheim, even with Prohibition in place it was impera-tive to ensure that a formerly "wet" populace remained truly dry.

Across the United States, the Invisible Empire—another name for the KKK—had four million members by 1920 and six million by 1924 at the height of its influence. Fraternal order-style secrecy, rituals, and discipline, subscribed to by a select group of white Protestants as dues-paying members, defined the KKK. From 1923–1925, rapidly increasing KKK membership gave would-be political operatives a base of support and provided opportunity to control government and exert influence.

In Anaheim, the tactic was to undermine the entrenched establishment. For years, descendents of the German founding families had determined city development, public building proj-ects, and provided boosterism to attract new residents. Those who responded to come-hither pitches, mostly Midwesterners, doubled Anaheim's population but were conservative, white, Protestant, and anti-Catholic. Dissenters who had been battling the estab-lishment status quo saw the new arrivals as supporters of reforms that would free the city. Strength in numbers, dissenters reasoned, would save Anaheim from hidebound free spenders and keep boot-leggers out. A moral majority could more firmly control the city's criminal elements that the police and citizens who were secretly KKK members were always saying were out there.

In spring 1922, Anaheim's first version of a Klan klavern appeared in a letter telling a hotel owner, a possible bootlegger, to leave town. Then an open letter appeared where the KKK assured law-abiding people that they were safe because the KKK would preserve law and order. A law enforcement raid in Ingleside in Los Angeles County seized the area's Klan membership list that showed that ten Klan members were from Anaheim. The Orange County district attorney had the list published in the newspaper. The public revelation was exactly what the secretive Klan didn't need. For a few months in Anaheim, nothing more was heard from the Klan. But the KKK had merely gone underground and was about to organize a new klavern.

Reverend Myers had arrived in town from Redlands in San Bernardino County late in 1922. He quickly publicized special events at his church, like a special visitor that turned out to be a group of robed and hooded Klansmen ceremonially making a donation with a letter that proclaimed the Klan as protectors. He started a Mens Bible Club that became the center and clandestine cover for his Exalted Cyclops' Klan organizing. One group watched where the members shopped to encourage patronizing only Klan member stores. Anyone who didn't was un-American and would be punished, members were told during one meeting.

Myers's strategy was to keep a low profile. When the Klan was in a position to move against the rich local elite, it would battle on the enemy's turf. It would recruit as new Klan members those who already belonged to multiple fraternal orders to capitalize on their already admirable civic involvement.

Exalted Cyclops Leon Myers quickly scoped out Ana-heimers' concerns. His own agenda was to maneuver his hand-picked klavern members and respected citizens into as many of the five city trustee positions as he could. Someday, maybe his people would be in the majority. Two trustee slots were open for the April 14, 1924, election. Suddenly two serving members indicated that they would not run again. If he could success-fully run KKK men for those four spots, the Klan would control the city council and its business. No one except the sworn-to-secrecy membership would know that the eminent citizens on the ballot were Klansmen.

The candidates' respectability was paramount. There must be no question that they were already well-known and active in the community. The men chosen included two ranchers, one of whom also served as a school board trustee; a grocery store owner; and a Masonic Lodge member from an important local family. A few people suspected what was going on and one paper, the *Anaheim Bulletin,* mentioned an "invisible menace," but most citizens who weren't Klan members were only concerned about a city govern-ment with sensible, grounded-seeming eminent citizens. Perhaps the set-in-their-ways incumbents who had built a new and unnecessary city hall would be tossed out by the voters.

Myers' grass-roots organizing was basic. Peer suggestions or pressure, even subtle through-the-lines threats, worked better than any visible KKK robe-and-hood activity. Normal gossip, suggestions that local reforms were needed, citing patriotism in daily activities like shopping (at Klan-owned stores), or asking questions about whether you really wanted Catholics there or doing that, worked best. It would be made to seem expedient to join the Klan even if one didn't feel strongly about Catholics, Prohibition, or where you shopped. The Klan was never to be mentioned. The approach was banal and invidious. Eventually, 1,280 out of about 11,000 Anaheim residents were on the Ku Klux Klan membership rolls.

The campaign heated up. Closeted Klan members criticized the mayor whose administration had been in office seven years and had concentrated on beautification and city infrastructure improvements. Mayor William Stark had built a new city hall in spite of opposition and had failed to fund water and sewer projects for struggling outer neighborhoods. Mayor Stark, a city trustee, ran on his record. The Klan wanted more, enforcement of a dry city and Christian moral code.

The Klan Four won handily. Lest they be allowed to govern unattended, the Anaheim Klan immediately sent a letter warning them that god-fearing clean living would be expected of them and enforced by almost one thousand men. City workers were quickly replaced by Klan members, and ten of eleven new officers hired to supplement the four-man police department were KKK men. Signs went up at entrances to town showing "KIGA," that members of the Invisible Order knew was "Klansman I Greet You."

Prohibition ordinances got stricter. No longer were slot machines permitted in Anaheim. Anyone whose street or curb wasn't tidy was subject to sanctions. Citizens were warned: Police will stop your car for even a minor infraction.

And the police enforcement was hard to miss. On-duty policemen sometimes wore their white KKK robes and hoods. Anaheim

Police Department history notes that Klan members were ready to shoot anyone who interfered with burning crosses, like the one set ablaze in front of St. Boniface Roman Catholic Church. The Klan was suddenly public and apparently in control. A photographer spotted four white-hooded and robed men in an open touring car with a sign on its side announcing KU KLUX KLAN LECTURE, 8PM TONIGHT, CHRISTIAN TABERNACLE, ANAHEIM.

For three months, the city trustees awarded jobs and tightened the laws. The KKK was out in the open now and making some citizens upset. Some men started carrying shotguns with them when they went outside, just in case. The Klan started compiling a list of 299 vocal anti-Klan activists.

Meanwhile, advertising across Southern California announced a July 29 KKK rally and mass initiation at Anaheim's City Park that drew ten thousand members of the Invisible Empire. A parade, marching bands, and an airplane with crosses on the fuselage flying above the assemblage preceded the ceremony that took place around a huge glowing cross.

Anti-Klan citizens were worried and determined to get open government and the city back. Activists started organizing seriously in August, buying the Anaheim klavern membership list from a willing Klan official. When Klan members stood for California and Orange County offices in a late August primary election, the county district attorney did as he had done in 1922 when the Ingleside raid netted the KKK membership list. He gave the KKK membership list provided by the Anaheim anti-Klan activists to the press.

The anti-Klan campaign in Anaheim began in the newspapers and at informational meetings. Who are these men with a secret agenda dictated by the secretive Ku Klux Klan, these men who got elected as city trustees without disclosing that secret affiliation? There was overwhelming support for a citizens' petition protesting the city trustees' removal of a downtown flagpole. Fraternal organizations came out in opposition to the KKK. The anti-Klan activists' organization, named the U.S.A. Club (for Unity, Service, and Americanism), organized a petition signing for a recall election.

In the three months before the recall election on February 3, 1925, the U.S.A. Club and others who were anti-Klan had to make a case. They said that secretive government was wrong.

Reverend Myers suddenly seemed to be everywhere. Every ounce of charismatic, persuasive self-conviction was used to argue that everyone except the fifth city trustee was upholding the laws of the land. He was helped in the effort by the Klan-supporting *Orange County Plain Dealer.* "Mom, apple pie, and the American way"–style patriotism must be protected from anyone who dared to attack the Klan.

As the recall election date neared, the battle of words got fiercer. Meetings were held. Klan supporters praised the dry state of the town since the four city trustees had ordered crackdowns on (suspected) bootleggers. The U.S.A. Club hammered at the secretive city government, the opposite of what the law guaranteed.

Election day came and more than 77 percent of the eligible electorate turned out. The tide had turned against the Klan and the four Klan city trustees were recalled. The non-Klan city trustee remained in office. All but two members of the police force were fired, even after they had threatened that if they were let go, the community would be unprotected without police on duty.

Within four months, the newspapers had agreed to eliminate mention of the Ku Klux Klan. The *Plain Dealer* was acquired by one of its rivals. Distribution of flyers in public places in Anaheim was outlawed. Membership organizations would have to be approved before they could recruit members. The new city trustees panel warned in the newspapers that if Cyclops Myers organized their recall, any Klan members or sympathizers would lose their jobs.

Reverend Leon Leroy Myers resigned his church position and left town in December. Although the Ku Klux Klan lingered in Anaheim and elsewhere for the next decade, the KKK and its jerks who had co-opted control of where people shopped, how they drove, the state of sidewalk cleanliness, what their religion could be, and how dry citizens really were, would never again be able to secretly conspire to take over Anaheim's city government.

Sources

In *Invisible Empire in the West: Toward a New Historical Appraisal of the Ku Klux Klan of the 1920s,* edited by Shawn Lay (Urbana: University of Illinois Press, 1992), Leonard J. Moore writes an introductory chapter, "Historical Interpretations of the 1920s Klan: The Traditional View and Recent Revisions," while Christopher N. Cocoltchos's statistical and social research is laid out in "The Invisible Empire and the Search for the Orderly Community: The Ku Klux Klan in Anaheim, California." The online City of Anaheim Police Department's History for the 1920s labels the KKK infiltration of the department in 1924 as "poisonous" at www.anaheim.net/articlenew2222.asp?id=667. *Los Angeles Times* staffer Greg Hernandez asked older Anaheim residents what they knew from relatives about what had happened when they were just children in "It's Been 70 Years Since Anaheim Booted Klan" (November 26, 1994).

On March, 20, 2003, the *Los Angeles Times* reported that an eight-foot cross had been burned in the Anaheim Hills front yard of a black-Latina couple. In "Neighbors Decry Anaheim Cross Burning," staff writers Mai Tran and Mike Anton said that the incident that had shocked a neighborhood of people from diverse backgrounds was being investigated as a hate crime by local police and the FBI.

Much Ku Klux Klan activity concentrated on morals with an emphasis on discrimination against non-whites and Catholics. With a cover blurb, "DON'T BE HALF A MAN JOIN THE KLAN," the *San Diego Historical Society Quarterly* (Spring/Summer 2000, Vol. 46, Nos. 2 & 3) published Carlos M. Larralde and Richard Griswold del Castillo's article, "San Diego's Ku Klux Klan 1920–1980," documenting KKK racist actions and violence against Mexicans elsewhere in Southern California.

CHAPTER 16

No One Came Back
William Mulholland and the St. Francis Dam Collapse

As the 1920s roared on, rich with good times and plenty, Los Angeles built and built on its semi-arid desert landscape. The city sucked its one river dry. And hordes of new residents kept arriving.

In 1928, one man wasn't paying enough attention to signs that Los Angeles's most critical resource—its water supply—was in jeopardy. Something was very wrong with a crucial dam north of the city. The disaster that ensued was one of California's worst human-caused tragedies.

Citizens' need and developers' greed fixed blame on the multitudes who inhabited, owned, and grew Los Angeles. The disaster challenged Angelenos' confident dream of an eternal water supply. Negligence, arrogance, over-confidence, or whatever it was that drove the man in charge of Los Angeles's water supply to deny detected leaks in the dam, was of immense consequence to the communities that suffered. The tragedy abruptly finished the career of that bringer of water, William Mulholland, a jerk for causing woe he might have prevented. Singular among all the California jerks appearing in this book, Mulholland later took personal and sole responsibility for his behavior. One question remains: Can a jerk find redemption?

> *The dam disaster…yeah, people heard it. A wife was working down there, her husband went down to look for her, and he never came back. No one did.*
>
> —As remembered by Roger, a man from Santa Clarita

The chief, William Mulholland, stood with Harvey Van Norman, his assistant, on a cement slab. Photographers from Los Angeles and local Ventura County newspapers clicked the shutters on their cameras in unison. Frozen for the front pages and for history was a stunned, lost-looking Mulholland. In one night, under cover of darkness, the career of the architect of the Los Angeles Aqueduct had been swept away as surely as the dam on whose remnants they stood.

A few days earlier, on March 12, 1928, at 11:57 p.m., a dam had burst forty miles north of Los Angeles, its pent-up waters whooshing with explosive force through San Francisquito Canyon. Sweeping all away—people, homes, fields, and animals—the wall of water released from its concrete enclosure rushed through the Santa Clara Valley for five and one-half hours, fifty-four miles to the Pacific Ocean. Twelve billion gallons of liquid inundated sixty square miles one foot deep before the water drained into the sea.

The St. Francis Dam collapse was a deadly, property-destroying disaster of the first order. More than 450 people were dead or missing. *They never came back.*

For two months after the horrible event, the monolithic remnant resembling an ancient tomb that Mulholland and Van Norman had stood upon like rooted statues marked where the dam wall had been. The stark slab was called "The Tombstone," one of many concrete chunks and boulder-sized pieces of the destroyed dam that could be found downstream within one-half mile of the former dam site.

The cause of the disaster was the craving, the greed for the very water that had escaped to the Pacific, a water supply for the City of Los Angeles.

William Mulholland, the chief engineer of the Los Angeles Department of Water Power in 1928, loved water and loved engineering. As the designer and shepherd of the Los Angeles city water supply, his mission was to ensure enough would always be available for city residents. What no one anticipated when a young Mulholland got a ditch tender job with the city's then-private water company in 1878 was that the Los Angeles River and its channels and ditches would soon be unable to provide enough water for those citizens.

Born in Belfast, Ireland, in 1855 and raised in Dublin, Mulholland had some schooling before serving in the British Merchant Marine for four years. At nineteen, Mulholland left seafaring in New York City and eventually worked for Pennsylvania relatives. With them, he left by ship for the renowned healthier climate in Southern California, but as a stowaway, he was put off the ship and with a brother, walked across the Isthmus of Panama to save the $25 train fare.

By the time the Mulholland brothers reached Los Angeles in 1876, nine thousand residents of a dusty, still frontier-feeling pueblo were starting to drill deeper for artesian wells. Hired to hand-drill a well, Mulholland was fascinated by fossils brought up from six hundred feet down. He began to read about geology and decided to become an engineer.

After a brief prospecting stint in Arizona, Mulholland returned to Los Angeles and became a ditch tender for the Los Angeles Water Company, the private corporation that in 1868 had leased thirty years of water rights from the city. He learned, progressed, and taught himself by reading engineering and technical books from the Los Angeles Library. He looked at the river, the ditches, canals, wells, and reservoirs as he walked and moved around the city, memorizing them along with never-mapped underground pipe systems in a diagram in his head. The self-taught hydraulic engineer was thirty-one years old when he became the water company's superintendent in late 1886, chosen as the most qualified and knowledgeable man after his predecessor died of a heart attack.

Mulholland later said he fell in love with Los Angeles the first time he saw it.

Mulholland's expression was open, his blue eyes focused. People were impressed by his bearing, upright posture, and confidence. Perhaps from the years at sea, he got along well with men and later with his work crews, who sensed his innate ability to direct others without mincing words. He lived as his crews did, and sometimes with them "in the rough," not caring much for basic housekeeping. The handsome Irishman became a naturalized American citizen in 1886 and married in 1890. As before his marriage, he was often away at a construction site and on-call at any hour to trouble-shoot water system problems.

For years, Mulholland fixed pipes and situations where waterways burst, testified before commissions, in hearings, and to arbitration panels about the works, the volume of existing water, and how much would be needed for the future. He never criticized his bosses at the private water company but became known for stating his mind based on the knowledge he had gained. Disputes between the city and the water company over which would repair the irrigation systems, domestic water systems, and who would set water rates were endless.

Finally in 1899, the City of Los Angeles regained control of water within the city limits, at least technically. After litigation and fights over who owned water rights and equipment built by the private water corporation, in 1902, the city gained total public control of its water, with an approved bond measure to fund the private company buyout. William Mulholland transitioned from the private to public sector Los Angeles Department of Water, in the same job, with the same title, the only man who knew everything about the city's water.

Meanwhile, Los Angeles's population was booming. North of Los Angeles in the San Fernando Valley, not yet part of the city, was the source of the Los Angeles River. From 1868 to 1899, while the private Los Angeles Water Company had operated the city water system, I. N. Van Nuys and J. B. Lankershim had bought land in the valley. As the twentieth century began, a group of investors, including owners of the *Los Angeles Times,* and a member of the Los Angeles water board, quietly bought 108,000 acres of valley land.

Los Angeles's chamber of commerce widely promoted the city's fine weather and urged new residents to come live in homes in attractive new neighborhoods. Newcomers arrived, adding pressure to existing water system use. Los Angeles's growth, said Mulholland, meant looking for sources of water beyond the Los Angeles River.

Like Mulholland, Fred Eaton, son of the man who founded the Pasadena Colony and developed irrigation systems for his orange groves, was passionate about water. In 1876, the twenty-year-old Eaton became the Los Angeles Water Company superintending engineer. Ten years later, he was elected the city's engineer, and then served as mayor from 1898 to 1900, vowing to make the public water system viable and keep rates low. He left office vowing never to run again.

Joseph B. "J. B." Lippincott, an engineer, topographer, and hydrographer, was deeply involved with public and private clients' water cases and had worked for the state of California, US Geological Survey, and the City of Los Angeles. In 1902, the newly formed US Reclamation Service, authorized to remove lands from private use to encourage public uses like irrigation projects, hired Lippincott, the Los Angeles expert, as the supervising engineer for California. In an unusual arrangement, he was permitted to do private clients' work after regular hours.

Eaton and Lippincott were close friends. Eaton and Mulholland had worked together on water issues for years. In 1892, Eaton had started talking up a new water supply to run about 225 miles from the Owens River that ran down the Owens Valley in Eastern California. The region was agricultural, with crops, orchards, and cattle. The main landowner, a cattle rancher, owned most of Mono County. Reclamation Service Chief Engineer Lippincott went out to the Owens Valley in 1903, talking to farmers and settlers and telling them that reclamation was imminent. Some Owens Valley people signed away their water claims, as Lippincott gathered information about who owned what land.

By 1903, there were 175,000 Angelenos. Mulholland estimated that there would be 390,000 water consumers by 1925. He and the City of Los Angeles truly needed more water.

*William Mulholland, chief engineer, Los Angeles Department of Water
& Power, and Harvey Van Norman, Mulholland's deputy, inspecting the
wreckage at the St. Francis Dam site on March 15, 1928*
COURTESY SANTA CLARITA VALLEY HISTORICAL SOCIETY. *LOS ANGELES HERALD EXAMINER* PHOTO.

In summer 1904, Eaton and Lippincott were among campers enjoying the Sierra Nevada lakes and sights in Yosemite, at Mono Lake, and south along the Owens Valley. The hydraulic engineers looked at the landscape and talked about the land to be reclaimed and how to get its water. On his return to Los Angeles, Eaton convinced Mulholland to ride in a buckboard for two weeks to see the Owens Valley's potential for himself. When they arrived, Mulholland could conceptualize a completely gravity-fed aqueduct and various reservoirs that could be built to route water south along the valley and then over to and through the San Fernando Valley to Los Angeles.

When Eaton returned to the Owens Valley in March 1905, he went for dual purposes: an assignment from Lippincott to check on ownership of land where power generation rights might get in the way of the reclamation project, and, without announcing it, to buy up land and water rights for himself. He gave Owens Valley residents the impression that he was there only on Reclamation Service business. When residents caught on, Lippincott was investigated, then cleared of malfeasance but criticized for strange behavior. His reclamation plan recommendation languished, never acted upon by his boss, the secretary of the interior.

It took another year before Los Angeles got aqueduct approval from Congress and President Theodore Roosevelt, who had decided, despite personal appeals from Owens Valley residents, that, "it is a hundred or a thousand fold more important to the state and more valuable to the people as a whole if used by the city than if used by the people of the Owens Valley." In that year, 1906, Mulholland became the chief engineer for the Bureau of the Los Angeles Aqueduct.

Voters supported the aqueduct with bond measure approvals, including buying Eaton's purchased Owens Valley land and water rights. Residents were told that water would not be used for irrigation, but for Los Angeles household use and city maintenance.

Aqueduct construction began under Mulholland's supervision in 1908. His second-in-command was J. B. Lippincott, now assistant chief engineer of Aqueduct Construction. In five years, the massive 233-mile engineering and hydraulic project complete with three large reservoirs, was finished. Mulholland faced forty thousand spectators who had journeyed to see the inauguration of the Los Angeles Aqueduct at the Cascades in the San Fernando Valley on November 5, 1913. On his command, project engineers opened the flow valves and water flowed. "There it is, take it," said Mulholland.

The project did drain a lot of water from the Owens Valley and made Owens Lake a dry lakebed. Area farmers were outraged at the loss of water for their own irrigation ditches and at the prices they had been paid for land if they were willing to sell to Eaton, or later, to the City of Los Angeles. The aqueduct water was also irrigating orchards in the San Fernando Valley, allowing landowners there to profit. There were accusations that behind-the-scenes deals had arranged for Los Angeles taxpayers to fund rich men who had bought up the Fernando Valley and were now getting the aqueduct water. Meanwhile, Mulholland knew that Los Angeles's residential water supply was still not enough for more than four hundred thousand residents in 1913.

In 1911, anticipating that on the aqueduct opening day, the city's population would exceed his original estimate of 260,000 residents, Mulholland had chosen San Francisquito Canyon for another reservoir that would be contained by a dam. Aqueduct water would run alongside the canyon. A dozen years later, the dam became a necessity for Mulholland's mission to provide water. When the required site study for the St. Francis Dam was done in 1923, it was approved for a capacity of thirty thousand acre-feet (the water volume to cover an acre to a depth of one foot).

In 1924, as the first St. Francis Dam concrete was poured, Owens Valley residents had had enough of the Los Angeles Aqueduct, the increasing lack locally of available water, and low prices offered for their land. Ranchers and their families drove out from Bishop to the Alabama Gates (near the Alabama Hills that have served as background and sets for many movie Westerns) on November 16, 1924, and set up camp. During the five days they were there, the ranchers opened the gates to divert water from the Los Angeles Aqueduct into a spillway that drained back to the Owens River. The action made headlines. There were other incidents of dynamiting the aqueduct. To Mulholland, stopping the water flow by dynamiting was clearly sabotage. The need to have more secure water storage was becoming ever more urgent. In 1924, Mulholland adjusted the St. Francis Dam plans to add ten feet to its height and 2,000 acre-feet.

In 1925, Mulholland again increased the height of the St. Francis Dam by ten feet and added increased capacity to total 38,168 acre-feet. In March 1926, Los Angeles Aqueduct water began to pour into the reservoir. Two years later, the St. Francis Dam was at capacity. At a maximum height of 1,834.75 feet, the 38,168 acre-feet limit was reached on March 7, 1928.

That same day, the St. Francis Dam keeper who was in charge of safe operations reported to Mulholland that his inspection had spotted leaks. Local people later said that they could see the nearby roadbed sinking. Mulholland is said to have told the keeper that leaks were normal. On March 12, the dam keeper called Mulholland again to report more leaks. At noon, Mulholland and Van Norman, his assistant, arrived to inspect the dam. Mulholland said that the leaks they saw were normal for a concrete dam.

Less than twelve hours later, shortly after 11:57 p.m., Van Norman was on the phone line to the Mulholland household with the horrific news that the St. Francis Dam had burst. During the next five and one-half hours, the waters left up to seventy feet of mud in their path through the communities of Castaic Junction, Fillmore, Bardsdale, and Santa Paula, to Montalvo at the Pacific Ocean. The dam keeper, farm workers, laborers, school children, and residents, husbands, and wives, more than 450 souls in all, were drowned, pulled into the mud, or swept out to sea.

Mulholland said publicly that he envied those who had died. He stood still with Van Norman atop the concrete ruins, no longer erect, his eyes cast downward, captured in defeat by the news photographers' cameras.

Swift investigations and later reviews of construction methods and the dam site's geology arrived at multiple explanations for the dam failure. There was evidence that there had been landslides on the earthen side of the dam. Perhaps the types of soils weren't proper or properly drained to support the dam structure and allow for pressure relief? The dam's height had been increased several times from inception to completion, perhaps adding pressure and stress with added water volume. Some experts thought that dam base supports were not large enough. Engineers noted that there was no inspection or drainage tunnel inside the dam, nor trenches to deflect or cut off potential water overflows. Like San Francisco, a municipality that was exempt under California law from required engineering inspections for its Hetch Hetchy Valley inundation for the O'Shaughnessy Dam in Yosemite National Park, Los Angeles's municipal water projects also weren't subject to inspection by state or outside authorities. The state engineer had visited briefly one afternoon.

"We overlooked something here," Mulholland told a Los Angeles County coroner's inquest later in March, although he never elaborated on what was missing. "Don't blame anyone else, you just fasten it on me. If there is an error of human judgment, I was the human."

The coroner's report concluded that the dam collapse was caused by a paleomegalandslide behind the dam's eastern abutment and noted that geologists and geological methods in existence at the time could not have detected problems when the dam was being built. Mulholland was cleared of charges of responsibility for the disaster, although the inquest concluded that, "construction and operation of a great dam should never be left to the sole judgment of one man, no matter how eminent."

Mulholland retired a few months later but not before ordering that the water level of the Hollywood Reservoir behind the Mulholland Dam be reduced. The chief engineer, already consulting on the Boulder Canyon (Hoover Dam) project, part of the Colorado River Aqueduct that would bring even more water from the Colorado River to the City of Los Angeles, saw his long career shattered. Friends and colleagues remarked that Mulholland seemed sad, a changed man. He left public life and remained secluded with his family until he died in 1935. His memory was honored as his body lay in state in the gleaming white city hall building of the city he had served. But William Mulholland never recovered from the tragic deaths of *those who never came back*.

POSTSCRIPT: REDEMPTION

The St. Francis Dam failure is the hydraulic version of an epi-center of water optimism shattered by geology and human fail-ure to take into account the mechanics of building structures atop California's tenuous soils. Time has erased most signs of the force of the water wave. The Santa Clara Valley is built up and Santa Clarita (actual site of the dam) is now best known as the home of Six Flags® Magic Mountain amusement park.

Los Angeles's water requirements continued to grow. A second, 137-mile Los Angeles Aqueduct that paralleled Mulholland's origi-nal aqueduct for some distance, was constructed in the Owens Val-ley in 1970. Owens Valley farms and ranches had mostly failed by the late 1920s. Population decreased quickly due to dry lakebeds such as Owens Lake, a lack of water, and the prosecution of the ranchers' protest leaders, bankers who had funded many valley enterprises, on charges of embezzlement.

The great drying up of another lake appeared imminent. Mono Lake, north of the Los Angeles Aqueduct and east over the Sierra Nevada from Yosemite National Park, has water tributaries that drain *into* it, but there is no natural outflow. Beginning in 1941, the Los Angeles Department of Water & Power (LADWP) started tak-ing water from the tributary streams. The result was a dramatic lowering of the lake water level and the emergence of tufa towers, spiky porous limestone created by calcium carbonate. Naturally saline (salty), the lake's eco-system wasn't being fed with fresh mountain runoff. Millions of migrating California seagulls weren't finding land to protect them from predators as they arrived each summer to feed and breed. Ducks and geese disappeared. Alkali dust storms were frequent.

In 1968, university students and academics, led by David Gaines, formed the Mono Lake Committee that spearheaded scientific research into what was happening to the lake. One major goal was to limit water diversions to levels that were not environmentally destructive. Multiple rounds of litigation against LADWP by the Mono Lake Committee, National Audubon Society, California Trout, and other groups resulted in a 1983 California Supreme Court decision that the state must use public trust criteria to grant resource allocations—including Mono Lake. In 1994, the landmark California Water Resources Control Board Decision, D-1631, ordered that LADWP water diversion must protect the public trust and that lake levels would have to be raised to 6,392 feet. In 1997, both sides negotiated a settlement agreement providing for restoration of Mono Lake and its streams, with diversion of water to Los Angeles based on lake level and successful restoration. Angelenos began to conserve water. The Mono Lake Committee website (monolake.org) now charts the exact water level: historic high and low, litigated level, and level-to-date. If there is salvation at the end of this tale of watery greed, the restoration of Mono Lake may be the redemption.

SOURCES

Catherine Mulholland writes about her grandfather's life in *William Mulholland and the Rise of Los Angeles* (Berkeley: University of California Press, 2000), with compassion for "the Chief" and a biographer's attention to detail without whitewashing the uncomfortable incidents. Parimal Rohit describes the history of the dam and its failure for the local newspaper, *The Santa Clarita Valley Signal,* in "Remembering the St. Francis Dam—80 years later" (the-signal.com/archives/677), updated on May 8, 2008. Two history professors, Donald C. Jackson and Norris Hundley Jr., review geology, design, and construction methods in prior dam disaster studies in "Privilege and Responsibility: William Mulholland and the St. Francis Dam Disaster" for *California History* (Vol. 82, No. 3, 2004).

Water issues are at the center of Mulholland's story and life. *Water and Power: The Conflict over Los Angeles' Water Supply in the Owens Valley* (Berkeley: University of California Press, 1982), by William L. Kahrl, lucidly covers Los Angeles's, Eaton's, and Mulholland's strategy to develop the burgeoning metropolis water supply, ending while a second aqueduct from Mono Lake was still in litigation. A definitive summary, it lays out the case for California as "a state inventing itself with water." Mark Reisner's *A Dangerous Place: California's Unsettling Fate* (New York: Pantheon Books, 2003) expands on California's and Los Angeles's dire water handling, first explained with reference to the Owens River Valley and the St. Francis Dam disaster in his seminal book, *Cadillac Desert* (revised and updated edition, New York: Penguin Books, 1993). Historian, activist, and commentator, Carey McWilliams, describes Los Angeles's obsession with water and the effects on the state's and national water policy in his 1946 essay, "Water! Water! Water!" in *Fool's Paradise: A Carey McWilliams Reader,* edited by Dean Stewart and Jeannine Gendar (Berkeley: Heyday Books, 2001). The Los Angeles Department of Water Power website (ladwp.com) covers high points of aqueduct history.

Professor Steven N. Ward, research geophysicist, earth and planetary sciences, at the University of California, Santa Cruz, shows the simulated progress of the disaster flow interspersed with contemporary photographs in a video, *1928 St. Francis Dam Collapse and Flood Simulation* on his website (http://es.ucsc.edu/~ward/).

Dropping the reader alongside young Ventura photographer Leslie White who takes his camera to trace and document the flood path from the Pacific back to the ruined dam site, Richard Rayner's *A Bright and Guilty Place* (New York: Doubleday, 2009) evokes the horror of the disaster. In Rayner's "narrative nonfiction," White's subsequent brief but significant stint with the Los Angeles Police Department as a detective (he also photographs Ned Doheny's murder—see the Teapot Dome chapter) parallels a local Los Angeles con man's corrupt spiral downward in a *noir* atmosphere in the style of real-life mystery writer Raymond Chandler.

Index